HISTORIC
MILWAUKEE
PUBLIC SCHOOLHOUSES

HISTORIC
MILWAUKEE
PUBLIC SCHOOLHOUSES

Robert Tanzilo

FOREWORD BY GREGORY E. THORNTON

Charleston | London

THE
History
PRESS

Published by The History Press
Charleston, SC 29403
www.historypress.net

Some portions of this work were previously published, sometimes in altered form, on OnMilwaukee.com, which reserves its rights.

The charts in the appendix are excerpted from *Our Roots Grow Deep*, 2nd edition, 1836–1967. © 1974 Milwaukee Board of School Directors. Certain photographs of MPS schools included in this work are owned by the Milwaukee Board of School Directors. Permission to use this material was granted by the Milwaukee Board of School Directors, which reserves all rights in the material.

Please support public education by making a donation at DonorsChoose.org or by volunteering your time at your local school.

First published 2012

Manufactured in the United States

ISBN 978.1.60949.780.4

Library of Congress CIP data applied for.

For Mr. Jack Pepper of Brooklyn, New York, and to all of his fellow public school teachers, because as lovely as schoolhouses can be, bricks don't make a school—teachers and their students do.

Contents

Foreword, by Dr. Gregory E. Thornton   9
Preface: What Schools Mean to Us   11
Acknowledgements   17

A Brief History of Milwaukee's Public Schools   19
Quiet Garfield Avenue School Is an Architectural Treasure   39
1891 Walker's Point School Salutes Albert Kagel   45
Brown Street to Groppi High   49
Twins, Triplets and Even Quadruplets in Vintage
     Milwaukee Schoolhouses   55
A Closer Look at Neeskara   63
Tracing the Decades at Maryland Avenue School   67
High Schools Carve a Special Place in Our Memories   79
Bay View Feared Closure of Mound Street School   103
Potter's Legacy Lives On at Gaenslen School   111
Looking At, and Into, Trowbridge Street School   117
Architectural Gems "Haunted" by Schoolhouse Echoes   121
Up in Smoke: Three Buildings Lost to Fire   125
New Uses for Old Schools   131
The State of Milwaukee's Vintage Schoolhouses   137
Lost Milwaukee Schoolhouse Treasures   143
Ten Must-See Milwaukee Schoolhouses   147

Appendix: MPS Charts   153
About the Author   187

FOREWORD

W ho doesn't love a schoolhouse? There are images of an old school that come to mind for most of us—at least for those of us who grew up in the age when school buildings were solid things of brick and stone and soaring panes of glass. I have spent the whole of my working life in such school buildings. There is a great comfort for me in a shiny terrazzo floor and in the gleam of an oak door that is worn from the touch of thousands of tiny hands, as well as in the brass knob of a classroom door that is all bright and shiny and ready to tell its stories, if only it could.

There is a different perspective that comes from being at the helm of a large public district with more than 160 school buildings in a variety of styles, some built in the 1890s and a few erected in just the past ten years. Each building is the setting of many thousands of precious memories for the children who attended there—children who are now grown and have moved on. They still want to see the old buildings in their old neighborhoods when they come back to town. Those of us in the administration of public school districts are as much the caretakers of structures as of students.

Robert Tanzilo clearly values the memories as much as he loves the architectural discussion. He explores the value of school buildings to the fabric of the city's neighborhoods with as much fascination as he explores boiler rooms and attics in our most elderly structures. This book relies on early documentation of the physical footprint of Milwaukee Public Schools (MPS) as published in *Our Roots Grow Deep*, a district journal that, unfortunately, captures history only up to 1967. We have been wanting more. We are grateful for the additional effort in these pages to nail down the past and present state of our MPS houses. They are integral to this city's future, creating long-lasting images based in brick, stone and glass for generations to come.

Gregory E. Thornton, EdD
Superintendent, Milwaukee Public Schools
June 2012

WHAT SCHOOLS MEAN TO US

G rowing up, my brother and I went to our neighborhood schools. As far as I can tell, there wasn't much discussion. Brooklyn's PS 199 was closest to our home, and so we enrolled there (or rather where District 21 enrolled us). We spent seven years in the circa 1920s, flat-roofed, red brick, three-story, U-shaped school, the wings of which engulfed the schoolyard and formed it into a capital "T," more or less. Every day for ten months a year, for those seven years from age five to twelve, we were in the classrooms, the hallways, the gym, the lunch room, the auditorium and the schoolyard at PS 199.

Is it any surprise that we feel a connection to our schools? Here we learn to read, write and create social bonds of all kinds. It is potentially the scene of our first crush (and the second and third). It is where we learn to create ourselves, out of the shadow and the close watch of our parents. It is where someone other than our parents or a close friend or relative mentors us for the first time. We walked to school every day, trudging through the snow and shuffling through the autumn leaves on the sidewalk, re-creating the sound of a train. PS 199 was as much a part of us as our house, our block or our friends.

We learned in most of the classrooms at some point across all those years. We stopped in the office and were in the gym and the auditorium every week, as well as the lunchroom and the fenced-in yard, with its faded painted lines.

At the same time, there were places at school we never visited. Those doors on either side of the south wall of the gym? Where did they lead? There were locker rooms up there, but we never used them. They were used

Kids mugging for the camera at Brown Street School, Twentieth and Brown Streets, as an addition to the 1898 building is erected in June 1952.

for storage, and the one time I can remember going in there, I felt like an archaeologist entering an Egyptian tomb. From one of my stations while serving as a door monitor I could see through the small pane of glass in the door leading to the bomb shelter beneath auditorium stage, but I never entered that mysterious space. We had climbed the caged-in staircases all the way up to the third floor by the time we reached the sixth grade, but in all those years, we never got to descend the same stairways to the locked doors of the basement. If you were lucky, you caught a glimpse while the janitor had the door open, perhaps moving his cleaning equipment in or out. What on earth was down there, and why didn't they want us to see it? Even at that young age, I had already stumbled on the mystique and the emotional strength of schools.

In his 1989 article "Cathedral of Culture: The Schoolhouse in American Educational Thought and Practice Since 1820," published in *History of Education Quarterly*, William W. Cutler III wrote:

> *The schoolhouse is synonymous with education and a reminder to all of an important time in their lives…More than 150 years ago reformers and educators*

in the United States began to claim that the schoolhouse was fundamental to the education of the young. One of the most prominent school reformers of the nineteenth century, Henry Barnard, insisted that the "schoolhouse should be a temple, consecrated in prayer to the physical, intellectual and moral culture of every child." His sentiments were hardly unique.

Perhaps oddly, perhaps not, I feel more enthralled by schools now that I don't attend them. Ask my mom and she'll tell you that I wasn't all that eager to go to PS 199 for at least a few years, despite the fact that I liked most of my teachers, had a fair number of friends and, as you can see, have a lot of fond memories of school. But for my entire adult life, schools have had an allure for me. Except that I don't think I'd make a good teacher, I'd consider that attraction to be a sign that I'm being called to the profession.

When my own kids started school in Milwaukee, I was immediately transported back in time. Although their school is much older than my elementary school, and though they look nothing alike, the scent is the same. I think it's the shellac on the creaky hardwood floors—as shiny on the first day of school as a freshly polished pair of patent leather shoes.

The effect was to fall in love immediately. I had a glancing history in the past with the building that is a major anchor and landmark in a neighborhood in which I've lived and spent a lot of time. I played basketball (if you can call my nonexistent skills "playing basketball") in the yard, and I knew a few people who attended. But none of that really played in. I was simply enamored of the building's steep roof, its ornamental friezes and its mix of Romanesque Revival design with Queen Anne elements. It looked to me exactly the way a school should look.

Taking the kids to school daily made me start to notice other schools. Sure, I'd seen lots of them in my years living in the city, but I never really *looked* at them. I began to be struck by the obvious beauty of notables like Fourth Street School (now Golda Meir School) and the now dark and empty Garfield Avenue School. I learned that they were not created offhandedly by some anonymous city architect. No, these two buildings were designed by Henry C. Koch, who created Milwaukee landmarks like city hall, the Pfister Hotel and Turner Hall. Milwaukee took its schoolhouses seriously, and more than a century later, it was still obvious to anyone willing to look. Surely, other cities have lovely old schools, but I doubt there are many that can boast of more gorgeous old schoolhouses than Milwaukee.

Many survive here, but others have been lost to urban renewal, fire and changes in educational needs that required the replacement of inadequate

The playground at Jefferson School, now razed, in downtown Milwaukee. It wasn't until the 1920s that Milwaukee Public Schools ensured that all schools had adequate outdoor play space.

old buildings. And this loss will continue. Every year, a deadly cocktail of declining enrollment and slashed funding forces Milwaukee Public Schools to merge schools and close buildings. Being active in a school community that inhabits one of the oldest schoolhouses in the city, I intimately understand the shortcomings. Our building is stunning on the outside. Inside, the too few classrooms are cramped despite the high ceilings. Because they weren't designed for today's students, the buildings are technologically challenged and often don't meet the specifications for accessibility according to the Americans with Disabilities Act.

As schools need to grow, the discussions begin. Does it pay to continue to expand and keep up a 125-year-old building? Will that investment continue to pay dividends educationally? After all, vintage schoolhouses live in our hearts and memories and decorate our landscape, but they exist to do a very specific function: help educate our children. If they no longer can do that effectively, is it time to say goodbye?

In Milwaukee, some old schools have found new lives as apartments, day-care centers and private schools. Two buildings were recently the focus of projects that would transform them into neighborhood arts centers.

This book is not an attempt to tell the entire story of Milwaukee Public Schools. It's not even a chronological history of the buildings in the roughly 170-school, eighty-thousand-student district. Rather, it's sort of a guide to

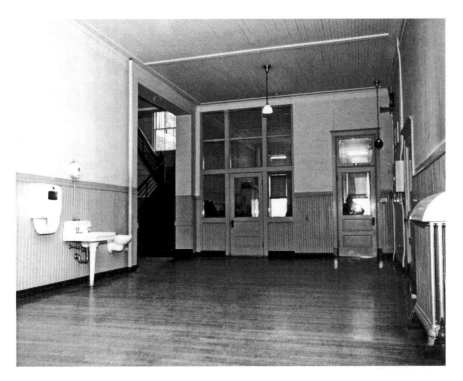

Vintage schoolhouses live in our hearts and memories and decorate our landscape, but they exist to do a very specific function: help educate our children. If they no longer can do that effectively, is it time to say goodbye? That was the case with the old Twenty-first Street School, seen here, which was replaced with a new building in 1978.

the discovery, or rediscovery, of some great Milwaukee buildings. I will pay homage to some long-lost schools, look at some veteran survivors and see how others are connected to their neighborhoods. We'll learn a little about some remarkable Milwaukee architects, too. We'll take a tour underground in one old school, and we'll go inside a few buildings that still stand but are currently empty.

We'll also look at what the future may hold for Milwaukee's old schoolhouses. I'm biased toward the oldest buildings in the district, and that bias will be apparent here. This is a catalogue of my admittedly amateur passion for these buildings, but I warn you: I'm not an architect. Some of you will know them considerably more intimately than I do. I hope that you find an old friend within these pages, and I hope that it helps rekindle some fond memories.

ACKNOWLEDGEMENTS

One rarely, if ever, writes a work of nonfiction alone. These are some of the folks who deserve some credit for helping create this one. Of course, I couldn't have spent the time on this project without the support of my family. Special thanks to them also for humoring me and not once telling me to clam up as I've pointed out old school buildings during our daily drives. A few chapters here originally appeared on OnMilwaukee.com, and I thank publisher Andy Tarnoff and site president Jeff Sherman not only for indulging my interests but also granting permission to reprint those pieces here, albeit sometimes in altered form. John Linn and Gina Spang in the Milwaukee Public Schools Facilities Department have gone above and beyond, answering questions and allowing me access to the district's archives.

Thanks to Dave Tesch for his architectural expertise and to Yance Marti for reading the manuscript and providing a slew of useful articles and advice. Thanks to Matt Cohen for showing me around the bowels of Maryland Avenue School and to Bob Hagner for his tours of some closed buildings. Thanks also to Milwaukee Public Schools superintendent Dr. Gregory Thornton for writing his thoughtful foreword during a busy school budget season and to Roseann St. Aubin, Amy Kant and the rest of the folks in the MPS Communications Department who offered answers and encouragement, too.

I owe a debt of gratitude also to MPS's Naomi Gubernick, the Milwaukee Board of School Directors and Lynne Sobczak and Eugene Jones in the Office of Board Governance. Thanks also to the staffs at the Milwaukee

County Historical Society research library and the special collections of the Milwaukee Public Library—especially Tom Stack in the Ready Reference Department and archives technician Gayle Ecklund—who helped me uncover some interesting photographs, architectural drawings and information. Ben Gibson, Katie Parry and the team at The History Press have again been a pleasure to work with.

A word on dates: MPS's own documents often list divergent construction dates for many of its buildings without explanation—perhaps based on groundbreakings, completions or school openings. However, the dates typically vary only by a year or two. It is therefore possible that some of the dates here will not match dates seen in other sources.

A Brief History of
Milwaukee's Public Schools

Milwaukee's public school history started in the winter of 1836, when the Juneautown settlement—one of three that would merge to create Milwaukee—opened a small frame school at what is now the southwest corner of Water Street and Wisconsin Avenue in response to Wisconsin territorial law that had been established that July. A few months later, Kilbourntown, west of the Milwaukee River, followed suit, opening a school at 371 Third Street, just north of what is now Kilbourn Avenue.

MPS's own history, *Our Roots Grow Deep*, quotes a longtime district principal, Patrick Donnelly, as saying, "The first schools were essentially primitive…a crude log hut or rickety frame shanty, 30 feet long by 20 feet wide, with a door in one end, a fireplace and chimney on the opposite end, four small windows…There was a wooden floor, long benches placed along the sides of the walls for the smaller children, and two or three small tables with appropriate benches for the more advanced pupils, who were able to write… Classes there were none. The variety book supply rendered it impossible to have classes."

By 1845, as the combined villages founded by Solomon Juneau, Byron Kilbourn and George Walker were working to consolidate into the single city of Milwaukee, *Milwaukee Sentinel* editor Rufus King was banging the drum for school expansion. "The whole number of school children between the ages of 5 and 16 years in the town of Milwaukee, is 1,781," he said, according to *Our Roots*. "There are 13 schools in operation within the corporate limits, viz., four public schools and nine private schools. Actual attendance at the public schools, 288; at the private schools, 356…There are upward of 1,000 children for whom no adequate provision of school accommodation is made. There are but two public school houses under this board, one of them hardly deserving the name."

The following year, Milwaukee was incorporated as a city, and a school board was formed, with King as president. By the end of the year, according to *Our Roots Grow Deep*, Milwaukee had six public schools: First Ward, located in the basement of St. Peter's Catholic Cathedral on State Street; the Second and Fifth Ward schools, run out of old schoolhouses; and the Third Ward and the Fourth Ward schools, which convened in rented houses. A second Third Ward school was opened later in the year.

In 1847, the city had five districts and added three more schools, and by the following year, MPS had 865 students enrolled and an average daily attendance of 640 pupils. A decade later, the board authorized three high schools, although only two were opened. Those had closed by 1860 due to financial woes within the district.

A description of one of these early school buildings appears in the 1979 booklet *Toward a History of Eighth Street School*, written by Beth Green, Brian Kreuziger, Clare Look, Rachel Nardin and Jim Jaeger. The Fourth Ward School was built in 1850 on the site of the current Eighth Street School, at Eighth and Michigan in the heart of downtown Milwaukee. Their narrative offers some insight into not only what the buildings looked like but also how quickly they became obsolete in the ever-growing Milwaukee, which by 1850 was home to more than twenty thousand souls:

> *The first school on this site was 42 by 60 feet and cost $3,492.70* [roughly $81,000 in today's dollars] *furnished to house 350 students. The two-story brick building was divided into two areas on the first floor, each with an ante and recitation room for the primary and intermediate departments. The second story had one large room and two smaller ones for the grammar or senior department. The building was built by John A. Messinger…*[and] *opened in 1850…*[but] *probably not finished or properly furnished until about a year or so later.*

Interestingly, the building had a short life span. A replacement was erected on the same site in 1857. The authors of the Eighth Street School history noted that no records explaining the short life span were found, but they posited that it had quickly become obsolete—"the early buildings were built so cheaply," they wrote—or that it might have fallen victim to fire or "some other disaster." But the new building was definitely larger, so the reason for the replacement may simply have been an attempt to meet growing enrollment demands.

Fortunately, thanks to the *Milwaukee Sentinel* of July 15, 1857, we also have a description of the new building, which was the work of architects Mygatt and Schmidtner:

> *The building stands 75 by 45 feet…is three stories high and is brick and the style of the architecture is appropriate and handsome. On each of the three stories is a big room, 43 by 51 feet, with two recitation rooms* [each 12 by 18 feet] *connected with it. The room on the first floor is intended for the primary department, is 10½ feet in the clear, and will accommodate about 200 children. The second story, which is intended for the Intermediate Department is 11½ feet clear and seats about 150 children. The upper story, which is 16 feet clear, will be occupied by the principal department, there being separate desks and seats for about 130 pupils.*
>
> *Two wide and substantial flights of stairs, one on the right and left of the main entrance* [which fronts Eighth Street] *lead up from the ground floor to the upper story. Two similar and separate staircases in the rear lead down from the different stories to the out buildings, which are distinct from each other and cannot be entered from the outside. The school rooms are furnished with new handsome and convenient desks and seats, manufactured by Buffolo, the standards being of iron and woodwork of cherry. A slightly raised platform at the eastern end of each room constitutes the throne of the teacher in charge. The whole building seems to have been put up in the most thorough and workmanlike style, and no detail has been neglected. Indeed, it is a job of which the contractors and the city may feel equally proud.*

Nevertheless, within four years, the building was, according to the Eighth Street history, "repaired to aid convenience and durability," and by 1863, it was already overcrowded, leading to the construction of an addition in 1866. A second, two-story brick addition followed in 1874. Just six years after that, MPS's annual report was already floating the idea of building a third school on the site:

> [Fourth Ward School] *is the oldest building now in use and it is rapidly reaching a condition when it will have to be thoroughly reconstructed or deserted. It has been remodeled internally several times; has had additions*

Eighth Street School, the third school to stand on the site at Eighth and Michigan Streets, was designed by Henry Koch and is the oldest MPS building still operating as a school. It is home to Project STAY, an alternative high school for at-risk students.

made to it; is insufficiently lighted and heated; has no provisions for ventilation; and has outside privies with the most imperfect sewerage. The rooms used for Primary grades are especially objectionable. The ceilings are too low, and the effects of wet weather are plainly visible upon the walls, on account of there being no excavation under the building...These statements, which have been put in their mildest form, amount to a condemnation of the building. There cannot be the least question as to its unsuitableness for school purposes. The only debatable point is, when the city can afford the money required for a new schoolhouse?

In autumn 1883, a fire broke out in the outhouses, and three months later, the building was closed and the classes moved to the Exposition Center on Sixth and Kilbourn (site of the current Milwaukee Theater), while the district erected a new building, designed by Henry C. Koch. That building currently stands on the site and is the oldest still in use in the MPS system. In addition to its longevity, the building is also one of the few among those of its era to have escaped the boxy additions added to most nineteenth-century schools in the middle of the following century.

The enrollment growth that caused these changes at Eighth Street forced the district to build, build, build over the next seven decades in a school construction boom that would be halted first by the Great Depression and then World War II. During these decades, municipalities were beginning to recognize the importance of these buildings—which, remember, Barnard suggested should be no less than "temples" of learning and culture—and their method of construction.

In 1910, West Virginia state superintendent of schools Morris Purdy Shawkey wrote in the book *School Architecture* that

> *school architecture is an art. Too often we make the mistake of supposing that any architect or carpenter is able to devise a suitable home for a school and all its activities. Many times our architects plan school buildings by taking into consideration proportions, gables, architectural effects, lumber, brick and stone, and either forget or fail to understand the children and their work—the very things for which the house should be erected. Those with professional knowledge concerning the requirements for a modern school house should prescribe the general standards, and from these let the architects determine the other features.*

In West Virginia, as in Milwaukee, early schoolhouses had become inadequate, according to Shawkey, but things were changing: "Although we still have entirely too many dilapidated old, beggarly, box-schoolhouses, with doors battered almost to destruction, windows small and broken, general appearance ragged, yards covered with a few abused bushes, weeds and 'blackberry vines,' they are marked for removal just as soon as financial conditions will permit. The 'beggars,' for the most part have given way to a better type."

Five years later, W.O. Thompson expressed similar sentiments on the importance of school design in his introduction to architect Wilbur T. Mills's 1915 book *American School Building Standards*. "The recent movements in education as effected by legislation have emphasized the physical plant as the basis of successful school practice," he wrote. "School architecture—including all the problems of safety, sanitation, heating, lighting, ventilation and others, having the physical well-being of the pupil in mind—has been the earnest study of many of the leading architects in the country."

This study and the seriousness of good school architecture were entirely appropriate, wrote Thompson (who declared public education to be the most important issue to the American people), because "the proper housing of the children during school hours, and adequate provision for play are vital to their future citizenship. Every effort looking toward the perfecting of school buildings should have cordial support."

A few pages later, Mills himself opined that "the school houses of any community are the gauges of its enlightenment" and that "one can hardly lay too much stress on the importance of highly skilled architectural or engineering services (or both) in the design and construction of school buildings. Any school building which is at all worthy of a competent architect's attention merits the services of the best man who can be induced to undertake the work."

Back in 1860s and '70s Milwaukee, things were looking up. In 1867, thanks to a law passed by the state, the city got a permanent high school. It was first located in the Seventh Ward School House and then in the First Ward School House. By the time it was about six years old, a fire drove the school to the Baptist church, and it later returned to the First Ward school building on the corner of Van Buren and Juneau (then Division) Streets.

In 1877, Milwaukee High School settled in at the then twelve-year-old Milwaukee Academy building on Cass and Knapp Streets, where there has been a school (currently Lincoln Middle School for the Arts, formerly Lincoln High School) ever since. By then, there were twenty-one public schools in the city, according to W.W. Coleman's *Milwaukee Illustrated: Its Trade, Commerce, Manufacturing Interests, Advantages as a Residence City*. Coleman was clearly a fan of some of them. "All of the latest improvements are found [at the First District School]," he wrote next to an illustration of the building. "And the interior is as complete and attractive as the reader can see the outside is."

Coleman also applauded the work of Henry Koch's firm with regard to Milwaukee's schools:

> *The matter of heat and ventilation has occupied the attention of the School Superintendent and Commissioners very much, and in the Thirteenth District school building, an illustration of which is here given, the subject has been practically settled...For which Messrs. H.C. Koch & Co., the architects, are to be thanked. The new building in the Fourteenth District, on Eighteenth Street, also planned by Koch & Co., speaks volumes for their ability...As architects for public school buildings, H.C. Koch & Co. are acknowledged to be leaders, not only in this city and state, but in other states, as was shown by the fact that they secured the contract for constructing the school building at Mt. Pulaski, Ill., over 74 other architects, representing nearly every state in the Union.*

Among Henry Koch's many school buildings was Eighteenth Street School, originally the Fourteenth District School, which was destroyed by fire in 1973.

In an 1875 address, then school board president Gustav Trumpff suggested that construction of school buildings—which, at the time, were uniformly named for the districts in which they were located (e.g., Eighteenth District School)—had continued apace in recent years. But the fact that the district did not control them was a hot-button issue:

> *A great deal of money has been expended by the city authorities for the erection of large and elegant school buildings…Still I believe that it would be wise to give the School Board a voice in the selection of sites for school buildings, and in determining their sizes and arrangements. When a short time since, the School Board, for the purpose of curtailing its expenditures, reduced the number of teachers in some of the schools, it was ascertained that most of our schoolhouses were planned without regard to the wants of the schools. Some buildings contain a number of small rooms, for each of which a separate teacher is necessary…during the winter the* [School Board] *asked for an amendment to the City Charter, providing that the plans for new school buildings should be submitted to the School Board for approval. The committee of the Common Council readily assented to this proposition, but no alteration was made in the law. This is much to be regretted.*

Twenty-seventh Street School, now home to James Groppi High School, was one of the many buildings erected during the tenure of MPS Superintendent William E. Anderson from 1883 to 1892.

In contrast to Trumpff's comment about small rooms, District Superintendent John Somers noted in his 1878 report that many classrooms "contain upwards of 100 pupils each." This fact might help account for why one of his successors, William E. Anderson, sparked a building boom from 1883 to 1892 during his nine-year tenure as superintendent. During Anderson's reign, the district built or annexed a large number of schools, including Clybourn Street, Dover Street, East High School, Eighth Street, Fifth Street, Fourth Street, Garfield Avenue, Highland Avenue, Hopkins Street, Lee Street, Longfellow, Madison Street, Maryland Avenue, McKinley, Mineral Street, Mound Street, Palmer Street, Park Street, Prairie Street, Sixteenth Avenue, Third Street, Trowbridge Street, Walnut Street and Windlake Avenue.

Others, like Vieau, Mitchell and Twenty-seventh Street and a very large expansion of Maryland Avenue, were completed within a year or two of his resignation in 1892. For this work, he would tap some of the city's most respected architects, including Henry Koch, Eugene Liebert and Herman Schnetzky.

Still, the district could barely keep up with enrollment growth. In the first weeks of 1893, Superintendent George Peckham told the *Milwaukee Journal* that twenty-six barracks were then in use to house an overflow of kids. Additionally, space had been rented by the school board to use as classrooms in the Sixth, Ninth, Thirteenth and Eighteenth Districts. "Not only is it necessary that buildings be supplied to take the place of the barracks but also that buildings be erected in the over-crowded districts," Peckham said. "The Fifth district is in great need of a new building. Pupils are packed into rooms in great numbers and even with that, many are unable to attend school."

The *Milwaukee Sentinel* noted on the first day of 1893 that the barracks were unfit places to educate kids, especially during Wisconsin winters: "These slightly built wooden structures are but insufficient protection against the severity of winter weather, and are poor places in which to attempt to keep school. But there is not the slightest doubt that the Board of Public Works will soon have to build several more of them so crowded are many of the regular buildings."

About $500,000 was needed by the district to build at minimum in the Fifth, Eighth, Tenth, Twelfth, Thirteenth and Fourteenth Districts but also in those districts renting rooms, Peckham said. "These figures are bedrock," he told the paper. "Not a dollar could be taken off the total. Yet even with that, the amount will be but sufficient for present necessities and when next year 1,000 and more pupils apply in excess of this year's number, the same difficulty will again be experienced...The money must be raised or else the practice of educating children made illegal, for matters cannot continue as they are."

Peckham said that the city's public works board and council were not to blame. What was needed was money, and for that the schools needed the state government to pay attention. "The legislature must be applied to," he urged, "[and] the power given to us to issue bonds." A delegation trekked to Madison that April to do just that.

The battle for elbow room in Milwaukee Public Schools wasn't showing any signs of going away, even as buildings continued to be erected. In an 1898 report, Superintendent Henry Siefert noted that while there were now forty-seven total schools (three high schools, twenty-four district schools, a school for the deaf and nineteen primary schools) and twenty-two one-room moveable schoolhouses, more than $500,000 would be required to meet building needs, which included five replacement buildings or renovations of existing buildings, five new buildings and additions to buildings in at least three districts. Plus, he said, a new high school was required to meet demand on the northwest side, and the Ninth District School that would later bear his name was in serious need of replacement:

I desire to call your attention to the unsatisfactory condition of the old Ninth District School. Some of the rooms are so poorly lighted and ventilated, that they should not be used as classrooms. Ten years ago, when I was principal of that school, I refused to use one of the rooms as a regular classroom, and had the seats taken out. Since then the clamor for additional school accommodations became so pressing that every one of the nineteen rooms in this building had to be occupied, and, in addition, two barracks had to be built. The new fourteen-room primary school on Twentieth and Brown streets relieved the pressure somewhat, but we could not take away the barracks.

A replacement in the Second Ward, on Seventh and Prairie (now Highland), was also urgent, according to Siefert, who wrote, "This building is without exception the poorest school building in the city. It has little or no provision for ventilation, except through the windows. The lighting is entirely inadequate. The basement is a dark hole." In the same report, Siefert bemoaned the lengthy process required to get a new school built. "Is it reasonable that it should take two years to build an eight-room school?" he asked.

Siefert did, however, celebrate the new buildings on Ring Street and Brown Street as advances in Milwaukee schoolhouse construction: "We may be justly proud of these last two buildings. They contain every desirable feature of a modern school house: proper size of rooms, correct lighting, steam heating regulated automatically, artificial ventilation and water closets on every floor." He also praised the forward-thinking mentality of building above current needs, writing, "Owing to the precaution exercised in building these two schools large enough, there are still five rooms vacant in one and one room in the other. If in the erection of new school buildings due regard be paid to the probable increase of the school population in the near future, we shall not suffer from the constant embarrassment of lack of school accommodation."

Yet, only two schools, the Seventh Ward (Jefferson) School and South High School, were erected in the following three years. After the nationwide depression of 1893–94 and recession that followed in 1895–97, money was tight in the second half of the 1890s in Milwaukee, and expenditures on school buildings were slowing.

In 1891, the city spent $244,000 on schools, but by eight years later, just $149,000 went to new schools. (The headline "Costly Buildings Scarce" was a recurring one in newspapers of the day.) And though the schools were erected, there was fear that there would be little cash on hand to furnish the buildings, according to a December 4, 1898 article in the *Sentinel*: "The fact that the city's finances are depleted will make no difference with the erection of these buildings [South High and Jefferson]. The money has been appropriated and is at hand. Some trouble may be experienced, however, in securing appropriations for the purchase of desks and other school furniture."

By the summer of 1899, the same paper noted that the lack of funds for school construction was hampering the district's ability to educate all of Milwaukee's children: "Only two new school buildings are to be opened in the autumn—the new South Side High and the Seventh District—and as these will do little towards relieving the pressure of an increasing school attendance, which even last year was too large for the accommodations, it seems likely that a good many children will find themselves crowded out for lack of room."

However, the paper noted, the district was working hard to maintain its existing buildings, and even that was proving difficult: "If the school board has not been able to erect new buildings for the accommodation of the children in the outskirts of the city, where the greatest need of more school room exists, it has been doing what it can to make the old buildings more habitable."

MPS spent between $8,000 and $9,000 to replace "unsanitary" plumbing systems in nearly a dozen schools, but that depleted the coffers and so talk of converting the old South Side High building into a primary school and other district-wide repairs and maintenance were put on hold pending a response to a district request for an extra $7,000 from the common council to do some of this work.

In 1901, the school board was still warning that buildings were overcrowded, and over the next decade, mostly under the superintendence of Carroll Pearse, construction picked up the pace. Between 1902 and 1911, a number of buildings were constructed, including Bartlett Avenue, Twentieth Street, Clarke Street, Auer Avenue, Siefert, Thirty-seventh Street, Ninth Street Annex, Doerfler, Forest Home Avenue, Lloyd Street and Thirty-eighth Street. One other, State Street, was annexed.

As early as February 20, 1898, the *Sentinel* reported that a predicted post-1900 school building boom was proving beneficial to architects. "The most important work among architects for the coming year is the drawing of plans for the numerous public schools that are to be built," it reported, noting that a site had already been selected for the District 18-2 building on Bartlett

Avenue and that plans had been made to raze the old school on Seventh and Prairie Streets and build a replacement and to build new schools in the Nineteenth and Twentieth Districts.

In a 1912 report, Pearse noted that during his tenure, he adopted a "policy of larger and better equipped school grounds, [a] policy of larger school buildings, rather than an increased number of smaller buildings, [and a] new type of school buildings with modern facilities and large assembly halls on [the] ground floor." (Earlier buildings typically had gyms and auditoriums—or more often "gymnatoriums"—on the top floor.)

A new penny-pinching approach appears to have taken hold, which may account for the reuse of plans for multiple buildings and for buildings less ornate or architecturally elaborate than their elder siblings. An example is the new First Ward School, built on Cass Street in 1905. As it prepared to open its doors for the first time, the school was described in a September 3 article in the *Milwaukee Sentinel*:

> *The new structure was designed with the main object of producing a building which shall be stable, sanitary and convenient in all its departments rather than one upon which money has been expended for the attainment of artistic results by means of architectural ornamentation. It was designed to be a straightforward and honest representation of a building which is practical in all its details. To this end the exterior is absolutely devoid of ornamentation and is impressive merely by its simplicity and straightforward expression of structural details.*

Under construction around the same time was the new Fourteenth District School—since renamed Rutherford B. Hayes—on South Tenth Street (then Fifth Avenue) between Hayes and Arthur (then called Smith and Clarence) Streets that the *Sentinel* reported on November 5, 1904, was the first steel and concrete public building completed in the city:

> *Walls, floors, stairs, columns, and roof are built of "reinforced concrete," which is concrete interlaced or supported with steel rods. When the building is finished it will appear to be made of brick, as there will be a veneering of four inches of brick. Behind the brick there will be a wall of concrete eight inches thick. Yet the walls, unlike those of a solid brick building, do not afford the chief support. There are concrete columns and girders, after the fashion of large steel structures. The columns of large size are 18x18 inches. A building of ordinary construction could not have an assembly*

Older readers will remember idyllic scenes like the one scene in this 1920s photograph of a kindergarten room at Harford Avenue School, which is still open adjacent to UW-Milwaukee campus on the east side.

room 48x66 feet in size without pillars to support the story above. Steel girders are used to avoid these annoying obstructions of the view, but in this building the concrete girders will be strong enough. There will be five across the ceiling [supporting] *the weight of the roof.*

In addition to the strength and fireproof qualities of this new type of construction, the *Sentinel* reported that "another advantage of the use of concrete is the cost," noting that while steel and concrete structures cost 10 percent more than frame buildings, they were 25 percent less expensive than brick or steel. The construction of Hayes—designed by O.C. Uehling—was projected to cost $60,000.

The school board finally wrested control of siting and construction of school buildings in 1905. The following year, the board, which by now oversaw fifty-one buildings, created an Architectural Division and hired D.C. Otteson—who had supervised the construction of Ferry & Clas's landmark Milwaukee Public Library, which opened in 1898—to run it.

In 1912, the board appointed Milwaukee architectural firm Van Ryn & DeGelleke as MPS architects on a half-time basis. For the next twelve years, the firm helped construct a number of buildings, most notably Washington, Riverside and Bay View High Schools. Also in 1912, the district again altered its schoolhouse nomenclature, leaving behind the old district numbering system because of changes to ward boundaries that followed expansion of the city. At its February 6 meeting, the board voted to name schools, noted Lamers, "according to the streets upon which they are located, the Superintendent and Secretary to select the names most desirable."

Lest you think the school board can undertake any action and avoid controversy, it's worth noting that even naming schools for the streets on which they are located drew criticism…six years later. In its June 9, 1918 edition, the *Milwaukee Journal* reported that the city health commissioner, comptroller and assistant city attorney all opposed the idea of street names on schools. "Naming a school after the street it faces does little to establish its location where is one or two others on the same street," it quoted the health commissioner, Dr. George C. Ruhland, as saying.

The article noted that Clybourn Street School is actually located on Twenty-seventh Street, and although there is one school named Twenty-seventh Street School, there is yet another school just few blocks north on the same street. The same problem existed on Ninth Street, Walnut Street and others, it reported. "Anyone who went to the school at Lee and Weil Streets in search of the Lee Street School would have to betake himself to Lee and Ninth Streets for that is where the Lee Street School is," added Ruhland. "Finding the Twentieth Street School deserves to be classed among outdoor sports, for there are three schools on Twentieth Street—one near Wright Street, one at Twentieth and Brown Streets, and one at Twentieth Street and Cold Spring Avenue. The first mentioned is the Twentieth Street School."

The paper asked Alderman Patrick J. Grogan—who was then lobbying to get a new school built to replace one damaged by fire in his Sixteenth Ward—if the schools ought to be named in honor of famous Americans as a means to teaching patriotism. "I think the lesson of patriotism ought to be taught in the class rooms," Grogan replied. "I believe that the system of naming the schools after the streets they face is so valuable from a practical standpoint that it should not be abolished." That opinion, wrote the *Journal*, was shared by Twenty-third Ward alderman John L. Bohn.

Otteson died in 1922, and in this same year MPS reorganized the Architectural Division, creating the Bureau of Buildings and Grounds. While it wouldn't hire a bureau chief until 1932, when it appointed Bohumil Jelinek, Minneapolis architect Guy E. Wiley was named assistant chief of the department and served as MPS's own full-time architect. Wiley would have a hand in the construction and expansion of many schools during his nearly thirty-year tenure in the district.

Further name tinkering took place in 1929, and while some schools kept their location-based names, others were given the names of artists, politicians, inventors, presidents, naturalists, writers and other notables. In June 1931, the school board's instruction committee made a decision that school leaders and educators could only have schools named for them ten years or more after their deaths. That meant the district had to delay the renaming of Ring Street for Robert M. La Follette and Third Street in honor of Victor L. Berger, and as the *Journal* reported, "[T]he naming of the new N. Sixteenth Street School after Emmanuel J. Philipp was also postponed in accordance with the 10-year rule." However, action was taken to rename the new North Stadium—still under construction—and the new nearby high school for Rufus King and to change the name of Clybourn Street School to Mary Hill in honor of a former principal.

After World War I, construction resumed, and during the 1920s, the district erected Bay View High School, Lincoln High School, Peckham Junior High, Roosevelt Junior High, Kilbourn Junior High, Kosciuszko Junior Trade, Fernwood, Franklin, Greenfield, Lapham Park Social Center, Neeskara, Riley, Sherman, Townsend, Wisconsin Avenue and the South Stadium. At the same time, many buildings were renovated or expanded, including Field, Fifth Street, Hi-Mount, Jackson, Mound, Palmer and Vieau, and many properties adjacent to schools were purchased to expand playgrounds.

"Many older schools had been built on small sites—'quarter squares'— and a program to provide adequate playgrounds for them in the '20s and for decades thereafter demanded the purchase and demolition of groups of houses," wrote William Lamers in *Our Roots Grow Deep.* "In thinly settled areas into which the city was expanding, large vacant tracts of land were purchased at acreage prices for immediate or future building."

The larger playgrounds were an acknowledgement not only of the importance to children of physical activity but also of the greater role schools played in neighborhoods. As citizens and civic groups began to push to fling open the doors of schoolhouses for other uses—including recreation, public meetings, social centers and other educational programs—the state legislature passed a law in 1907 to allow such uses.

In 1911 and 1912, MPS created an extension department, which opened social centers and playgrounds. At Detroit Street School in the Third Ward, a public natatorium was built in 1915 that offered vital services to a heavily Italian immigrant neighborhood. In October 2004, retired fifty-five-year veteran MPS

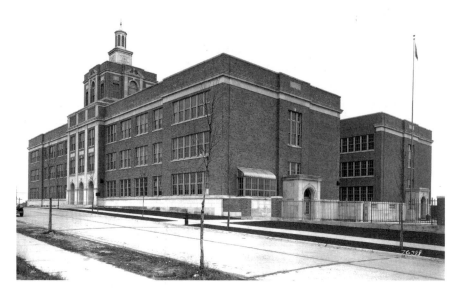

Steuben Junior High School on the west side was the work of Milwaukee Public Schools' resident architect Guy E. Wiley. Now home to the popular Milwaukee French Immersion School, the building retains its original tile work and other interior details.

educator Pauline (Eugenia) Stanwitt shared with Bob Ruggieri of the *Italian Times* newspaper her memories of the natatorium:

> *Few homes in the old Third Ward could boast of having a bathtub. In those days, a bath consisted of filling a round, galvanized washtub with clean hot water for each member of the family about to take a bath. This is how it was until the year 1915 when the natatorium was built. What a pleasure it was to enter the huge building and stand under the shower for a thorough washing before jumping into the blue/green water of the large swimming pool. Tuesday and Thursday was women's day. Wednesday, Friday and Saturday, the men took over.*

Construction in the district was stymied by the Great Depression, but by the end of the 1930s, the list of new construction, additions, renovations and major repairs was a long one. Burbank, Gaenslen, Garden Homes, Humboldt Park, Juneau, King, Morgandale, Philipp, Pulaski, Steuben, Story, Tippecanoe and the North Stadium were built, and more than sixty existing buildings were expanded or renovated or underwent major repair work. Wiley directed the bulk of the work in the 1920s and '30s, and by 1943, the district comprised 118 buildings and 22 playground buildings.

"Although this period was marked by considerable school construction," wrote Lamers, "the architectural staff carried almost the entire load of designing. By the late 1930s, as enrollments fell and funds grew scarcer, the building program slackened."

World War II brought construction to a full stop, and it did not begin again until a few years after the end of the conflict. After Pulaski High was opened in 1939, there was no new construction in the district until Eighty-first Street School was finished in 1949. Driven by demographic changes, that was a project, along with a few others, that caused the district to rethink its 1945 five-year facilities plan barely two years in.

"Shifts in Milwaukee's population have caused the school board to adopt a new five year building program, upsetting the program outlined in 1945 for its postwar construction and improvements," wrote reporter Elizabeth Maier Devitt in the *Milwaukee Journal* in November 1947. "Because of the rapid settlement of the northwest section of the city, the board has recognized elementary school expansion there as a first need and has pushed other projects further into the future." Among those newly urgent projects were the Eighty-first Street and Fifty-third Street Schools, along with improvements at Washington High School.

In the meantime, Jelinek had retired in 1942 (Wiley would resign in 1951). But times were changing anyway, and the postwar baby boom would force MPS to look outside the district for its architecture and design needs, according to Lamers:

> *To meet the building demands of the middle 1940s and the 1950s and 1960s, the Board was compelled to contract the services of local architectural firms. Under this arrangement the role of the Construction Division changed. It no longer planned and designed buildings and carried the construction responsibility through the whole cycle from blueprints to occupancy. It participated, rather, in the preliminary planning, assisted in drawing specifications and in selecting architectural firms for individual assignments, and followed construction—in a word, it was supervisory.*

With the lack of activity and the deferrals caused by rethinking the 1945 facilities plan, the district fell behind on modernization and construction projects, and in 1951, it floated a school bond referendum for the first time since 1926. The goal was to raise nearly $10.0 million, which would help fund $18.2 million in work to help erase what a report called "a critical housing shortage" for MPS. This shortfall, the district noted, was the result of an increasing birth rate, substantial growth in city population and aging school buildings.

The document attributes the rising age of schools to the decline in construction work during the Depression and World War II and to the fact that building costs had since increased without a similar increase in funding. In 1951, the district had ninety-eight buildings, with an average age of thirty-seven years. Twenty-two buildings were more than fifty years old, and three were more than seventy years old. Allen, built in 1875, was the oldest.

"While it has been the policy to keep these buildings in good repair, a program of modernization and probable replacement must be considered if we are to assure the safety and right of all children to equal educational opportunity," wrote Adell Schott in the school board's 1951 "Manual of Information: Future Needs of the Milwaukee Public Schools."

The district predicted a shift toward more high school–age students than elementary students in MPS. Not only would more high schools be needed, but those schools would also be more costly to construct. MPS also estimated enrollment, which had grown from 66,980 in 1948–49 to 67,409 the following year, would balloon to nearly 82,000 by the end of the decade.

Therefore, the "Manual" argued, the referendum simply had to pass, or Milwaukee students would be faced with the prospect of half-day school programs, long-distance transportation, increased class sizes, conversion of basements, auditoriums and other facilities into classrooms and "temporary construction [that] will be substituted for permanent construction with greatly increased maintenance cost and less educational service value."

Atop the MPS wish list? The construction of Clement Avenue School, Kluge School, Fifty-fifth Street School, Ninety-fifth Street School, a new West Division High School, improvements at Washington High, a new high school in the northwest part of the city and the remodeling and modernization of old buildings and barracks, or portable units, to alleviate overcrowding at some schools.

The second group of needs included a replacement for Allen and Field Schools (that building is indeed called Allen-Field), a replacement for Center Street and Pierce Schools and a "permanent unit building" for Curtin School on the south side.

On Tuesday, April 3, 1951, voters approved the bond issue by a 2:1 margin, and the projects just listed were completed. Eleven years later, the *Milwaukee Sentinel* reported that voters approved a $29 million bond offering to fund a five-year facilities plan.

"It was the fifth consecutive time since 1951 that Milwaukee had approved bond sales for new schools," wrote reporter Joe Botsford in 1962. "But it was the first time that a school bond proposal had faced such vigorous, vocal opposition. Civil rights groups fought the proposal to the final hours, charging that construction of schools in Negro populated areas would encourage further de facto segregation."

By 2011, when it completed its most recent facilities report, Milwaukee Public Schools—which has an enrollment of about eighty thousand—held 220 buildings and playfields in its portfolio and the average age had jumped to sixty-six years old. Just over 40 percent of the district's facilities dated to before 1930.

The report projected the total capital improvement need for the district's facilities to be $991.2 million. The oldest building still serving as an MPS school is Eighth Street, erected in 1884.

QUIET GARFIELD AVENUE SCHOOL IS AN ARCHITECTURAL TREASURE

When I drive past a building like the old Garfield Avenue School, 2215 North Fourth Street, which I do a few times each week, I'm intrigued. Garfield is an especially lovely old building that appears to still be in pretty good shape. Because it was in use from its construction in 1887 through 2006, it was maintained. That's a good thing because the building is a piece of Milwaukee architectural history. It was designed by Henry C. Koch, who is best known in town as the architect of city hall. Koch also designed Turner Hall, the Pfister Hotel, Marquette's Gesu Church and other buildings here and beyond.

Koch was a devotee of Romanesque Revival style and was a disciple of Boston architect Henry Hobson Richardson, the namesake of a style that came to be called Richardsonian Romanesque. Koch earned a number of school building commissions, including the early Fourteenth District School on Eighteenth and Wells and Detroit Street School (later Andrew Jackson), which were constructed in the 1870s, the Eighth Street and Maryland Avenue Schools in the 1880s and South Division High in the 1890s, among others.

Romanesque Revival/Richardsonian Romanesque was a popular architectural style in Milwaukee and across the country from about 1870 until about 1900. One of the most recognizable Romanesque Revival structures in Milwaukee is Willoughby J. Edbrooke's U.S. Post Office, Court House and Custom House (now the Federal Building on East Wisconsin Avenue), with its graceful multipointed tower, built between 1892 and 1899.

Garfield Avenue School was designed by Henry Koch, who designed such Milwaukee landmarks as city hall, Gesu Church and Turner Hall. Currently closed, it is on the National Register of Historic Places.

Other prominent extant examples include Edward Townsend Mix's St. Paul's Episcopal Church and, of course, Koch's Pfister Hotel.

Reflecting the open interpretation by nineteenth-century architects of eleventh- and twelfth-century western European architecture, Koch often blended styles, mixing elements of classicism, Palladianism, Queen Anne and other styles into his works.

KOCH, SCHNETZKY AND LIEBERT

As much as Milwaukeeans treasure some of the city's landmarks, few of us know much about the folks who created them.

Architect Henry Koch designed city hall—once among America's tallest buildings—Turner Hall, the Pfister, the "new" hospital at Milwaukee Soldiers Home and other great Cream City buildings. But does anyone beyond a small cadre of architecture students and geeks know his name?

Koch, who was born in 1841, designed more than three hundred buildings—including

fifteen courthouses in Wisconsin and Illinois and, reportedly, all Milwaukee Public Schools erected between 1873 and 1881 (and some afterward, too)—in a career that spanned forty years. Enlisting to fight in the Civil War, Koch worked as a draftsman on General Philip Sheridan's staff.

Even less known are Koch disciples Herman Schnetzky and Eugene Liebert, two German immigrants who, like Koch, arrived in Milwaukee and stayed to ply their trade. All of their best-known work was executed in the then fashionable Romanesque Revival style.

Schnetzky was born in Wriezen, Germany, in 1850 and arrived in Milwaukee eighteen years later. By 1869, he was working as a draftsman for architect George Mygatt—who, it has been suggested, was the first professional architect in Milwaukee—and his apprentice, Henry Koch.

Koch, who signed on with Mygatt when he was just sixteen, left to create a firm in partnership with Julius Hess one year later, and it is presumed that Schnetzky followed. But soon Koch was on his own. It was during these years that Schnetzky helped Koch design many early Milwaukee Public Schools. Eighth Street, Garfield Avenue, Fourth Street and Kagel are among the extant MPS buildings designed by Koch. Soon, Schnetzky was doing that kind of work, as well as other more prestigious commissions on his own.

In 1887, Schnetzky designed Greenfield School in West Allis. It was later renamed Garfield School and is currently home to the West Allis Historical Society. The Romanesque Revival schoolhouse was added to the National Register of Historic Places in 2006. In 1889, he drew plans for the nearly identical Walnut Street and Fifth Street Schools. He also designed St. Martini Lutheran Church (1520 South Sixteenth Street) in 1887, St. John's Lutheran Church (804 West Vliet Street) two years later and, in 1890, Blatz Brewing Company Office (1120 North Broadway) and the McGeoch Building (322 East Michigan Street). All of these are still standing.

In 1892, he went into partnership with his former Koch colleague Eugene Liebert. Born in Berlin in 1866, Liebert came to Milwaukee in 1883. His mother was a Gallun—as in the Trostel

and Gallun Tannery Galluns of Milwaukee—and he worked at the tannery until a partner there landed him a job in Koch's office.

Liebert joined Schnetzky as a draftsman in 1887, and they became partners five years later. That same year, they designed St. Michael's Church (1445 North Twenty-fourth Street) and, the following year, St. Stephen Lutheran School in Walker's Point (which still stands but is vacant), as well as a major addition to Koch's Maryland Avenue School.

But it was in 1896 that the duo drew the most enduring symbol of their legacy in Milwaukee: the Germania Building (135 West Wells Street). That same year, they produced plans for a new West Side (later West Division) High School.

In 1897, Schnetzky and Liebert parted ways, and each continued to build in Milwaukee. In 1900, the latter purchased land on the east bank of the Milwaukee River and built three distinctive summer homes and a lovely chalet-style barn. All still stand on Sunny Point Lane, though they are among sixteen homes that the City of Glendale is trying in 2012 to buy and raze.

Schnetzky died in 1916, and his son, Hugo, continued the family practice. Liebert died in 1945 in the home he designed and built for himself in 1887 at 1948 North Holton Street. Koch had passed away in 1910. According to Liebert's great-grandson, the family has made something of a tradition of Eugene's profession.

"He had four sons; two were architects—Walter and Carl—and the other two were engineers, including my grandfather, Arthur," said Rochester, New York–based architect Todd Liebert. "I am the only architect since Walter and Carl, with a practice that includes hospitals, schools and municipal buildings in both New York and North Carolina."

Maryland Avenue School, now a public Montessori school, has been an east side landmark for 125 years. The current building—erected in three phases in 1887 (Henry Koch), 1893 (Schnetzky & Liebert) and 1951 (Richard Philipp)—replaced a smaller First District Primary school located on the same site.

For a nice overview of Liebert's residential, commercial and ecclesiastical work, check out Milwaukee architectural historian H. Russell Zimmermann's book The Architecture of Eugene Liebert. You might be surprised how many of his works are still here, brightening up our landscape today.

Look at Turner, city hall and Garfield Avenue School—as well as Golda Meir School and its companion, Kagel School, also Koch works—and you will be struck by the commonalities: the arches over the windows, the peaks, the sets of triple windows and so on.

"The Garfield Avenue building was designed with a central hallway around which light filled rooms were grouped in irregular clusters," according to Built in Milwaukee: An Architectural View of the City, edited by Randy Garber. "The exterior of the structure was a late-nineteenth century caricature of Palladianism in that it was composed of three oddly asymmetrical masses. Furthermore, the masses were articulated by tripartite window systems, which were hugely overscaled. The impression given is that the building is lighter than it should be."

Garfield Avenue School, which was originally designated District 6-2 and also served as North Girls Junior Trade from 1936 to 1953, has been on the National Register of Historic Places since 1984.

1891 WALKER'S POINT SCHOOL SALUTES ALBERT KAGEL

Henry C. Koch also drew up plans for Kagel Elementary (1210 West Mineral Street) in Walker's Point. If you compare it to Golda Meir School (originally called Fourth Street School), you'll see so many similarities that it seems safe to say that Koch created both schools from the same basic design. Kagel (Mineral Street School) was built in 1891, the year after Fourth Street School was constructed.

Note that both schools have a central section with a trio of large arched windows—five smaller attic windows above and three insets above that. They are both flanked by symmetrical wings that repeat the "three arched windows" theme in sections that—like the central area—span the first and second floors. Above, a central arched window in each wing is flanked by sets of double windows. The central third-floor windows on each wing are topped with dormer peaks, with matching decorations. Both also share rough-hewn stone exposed basement foundations.

Some other schools from this era are of different design but share some similarities. For example, Maryland Avenue, built in 1887, shares the same quintuple window set at the attic level. Koch designed the original Maryland Avenue building, though a large addition in 1893 was the work of his disciples Herman Schnetzky and Eugene Liebert. While that school also has a rough-hewn stone foundation, it is not exposed. You have to enter the building to see it.

Maryland and Kagel share another connection. Kagel is named for longtime Milwaukee Public Schools principal Albert E. Kagel, who was the first principal

The former Mineral Street School in Walker's Point was renamed for longtime district teacher, principal and administrator Albert Kagel. The building, designed by Henry Koch, is a twin to Fourth Street School.

at Maryland Avenue, serving from 1887 (when the main part of the current building was constructed) until 1902. Kagel was born in Memel, Germany, in 1863 and arrived in Milwaukee seven years later. He attended Forest Home Avenue School (then Eleventh Ward School), and after graduating from the Milwaukee State Normal School in 1884, he was hired as a "grade assistant" and, in May 1885, was named principal at Fifth District Branch School.

In 1901, Kagel was made an assistant superintendent, a title he held until his death in 1923. He was acting superintendent in 1913–14. Mineral Street School—which was called District School 8-1 until 1912, when most schools got new monikers—was renamed in his honor in 1926. In 1928, after a fundraising campaign and push by educators, Milwaukee Public Library cleared space to create an Albert E. Kagel Memorial Room.

Milton C. Potter, who became superintendent in 1914, called Kagel "[a] man of inner kindliness, and therefore of simple courage," according to William M. Lamers in *Our Roots Grow Deep*. "A lover of little children, who feared no man, and therefore hated no man."

Fourth Street School, now renamed Golda Meir School in honor of its most famous alumna, is one of the most impressive buildings in the MPS portfolio today. The academic program is also one of the most respected and sought-after among Milwaukee schools. *Photo by author.*

Mineral Street School—like many other early extant school buildings—is part of the legacy of Superintendent William Anderson, who was top man at MPS from 1883 until 1892. Among the other buildings constructed during his tenure were Clybourn Street, Dover Street, East High (Lincoln), Eighth Street, Fifth Street, Fourth Street (Golda Meir), Garfield Avenue, Highland Avenue, Hopkins Street, Lee Street, Longfellow (Sixteenth Avenue), Madison Street, Maryland Avenue, McKinley, Mound Street, North Pierce Street, Palmer, Park Street, Prairie Street, Third Street (Victor Berger/Martin Luther King), Trowbridge, Twenty-first Street, Walnut Street and Windlake Avenue.

BROWN STREET TO GROPPI HIGH

It seems that quite a few people other than me are curious about and fascinated by old school buildings. My blogs about the Henry Koch–designed Garfield Avenue School and Kagel Elementary were well-received and drew a number of e-mails and in-person comments.

One teacher, for example, told me that Longfellow School, Trowbridge Street and Dover Street were the oldest extant public school buildings in the city. I'm sorry to tell this teacher that neither her school nor the others she mentioned can claim that distinction. Longfellow dates to 1886, Dover to 1890 and Trowbridge to 1894. That puts the first two right in the heart of the buildings erected during the tenure of Superintendent William Anderson.

While MPS's *Our Roots Grow Deep* notes that Trowbridge was built during the Anderson years, an Energy Star document that lists the construction dates of a number of district buildings gives the 1894 date. That, of course, could not be accurate if the building was indeed built during Anderson's time. Regardless, it is not the oldest.

The oldest, according to MPS facilities documents, is Brown Street School (2029 North Twentieth Street), supposedly constructed in 1882 But, MPS's own documents seem to be inaccurate on this point. The 1898 annual report by then superintendent Henry O.R. Siefert celebrates two new primary schools erected by the district in January of that year. One was on Ring Street (long since renamed LaFollette). The other was "a fourteen-room building replacing the old six-room frame building at the corner of Twentieth and Brown streets, in the Ninth Ward."

Opened as Ninth District Primary, Brown Street became District 9-2 in 1903 and was dubbed Brown Street in 1912, when many schools were renamed, typically after their locations. The street, and therefore the school, is named in honor of west side Milwaukee pioneer Deacon Samuel Brown.

The second is clearly a reference to Brown Street School, which stands on the corner of Twentieth and Brown. While it would seem unlikely that the district has misdated this building for decades (a 1940s facilities report also lists the 1882 date), it seems even less possible that Siefert, in a written report published by the Board of School Directors, got the location of this new construction wrong. A search in the MPS facilities archive did nothing to clear up this inaccuracy. If the latter date is true—and it likely is, considering that an 1896 edition of the *Milwaukee Journal* noted that numerous architectural firms had submitted competitive plans for a new building on Twentieth and Brown—then Eighth Street, built in 1884, is the oldest MPS school still in operation.

Opened as Ninth District Primary, Brown Street became District 9-2 in 1903 (when Siefert, 1547 North Fourteenth Street, opened) and was dubbed Brown Street in 1912, when many schools were renamed, typically after their locations. The street—and therefore the school—is named in honor of west side Milwaukee pioneer Deacon Samuel Brown.

The original building was already quite large, and it was later expanded to the north. Viewing it from the south elevation (Brown Street), you really get a sense for its orderly mass. Then compare it to nearby Siefert or a school like Golda Meir, and you can appreciate how spacious it must be in relation to other buildings of the era.

Like many others in MPS, Brown Street has a semicircular space. However, while some span two floors, the Brown Street half moon is only one story and appears to house a single room. Often these rooms were kindergarten classes, as was the case at Dover Street School, where the littlest pupils were taught in a half moon–shaped basement room flooded with light (thanks to its southern exposure) that illuminated a stunningly glossy oak floor.

An 1882 construction date would suggest that Brown Street was the work of Henry Koch, but the building lacks the adornment of the Koch buildings discussed in earlier chapters and looks more solid, like a weightier community structure. The absence of his style and the fact that it is stylistically similar to nearby Siefert Elementary, built in 1903, further suggest that 1898 is the correct date. The building was, in fact, designed by architects Henry P. Mollerus Jr. and Henry G. Lotter, who also designed additions to the Twentieth District School and to the Fifteenth District School in the 1890s. Lotter designed buildings vaguely similar to Brown Street for Clarke Street and Fratney Street Schools.

Siefert, named for MPS superintendent Henry O.R. Siefert (1896–1904) and built on a U-shaped plan, is similarly unadorned, although its central section boasts a lovely row of seven large arched windows on the third floor, giving it a Romanesque feel.

Siefert was opened in 1903 as Ninth District No. 1, a K-8 school, and a history on the school's website notes that the "student body was composed primarily of students from blue-collar German families. Pancratius Tiefenthaler [there is a Tiefenthaler Park nearby on Cherry Street] was the first administrator, and he served in this capacity for three years." I'm not sure if it was old Pancratius or one of his ten successors (including Siefert himself, who was principal of the school from 1906 to 1922) who was responsible, but I'd love to know why every one of the dozens of windows in the western elevation has been bricked up.

Like Brown, Siefert has a much later addition, too. But while Brown's is harmonious, Siefert's is a single-story utilitarian shoebox of an add-on. (It should be added, though, that Brown Street also has two other additions that are no treat for the eyes, either, and that Siefert has an earlier addition that is nearly undetectable to the naked eye.)

Also in the neighborhood is the former McKinley School (2001 West Vliet Street), which is now home to the V.E. Carter Human Resources Center. The

Siefert, on Fourteenth and Galena Streets, opened in 1903 as Ninth District No. 1, a K-8 school, and a history on the school's website notes that the "student body was composed primarily of students from blue-collar German families. Pancratius Tiefenthaler was the first administrator, and he served in this capacity for three years."

sprawling, now-painted Neoclassical brick building—which appears from the outside to be in need of some serious maintenance—was opened in 1885 as Fifteenth District No. 1 and was renamed Cold Spring Avenue in 1912. In 1927, it was named for the twenty-fifth president, William B. McKinley.

It's such a seemingly randomly arrayed amalgam of sections that it seems obvious it had been a much smaller building that was added onto a long time ago. The main section (the eastern part) was designed by Walter A. Holbrook. The west wing, facing Twenty-first Street, was designed by Mollerus and Lotter and was constructed in 1898 as an addition that is, in fact, an entirely separate building. Viewed from above (thank you, Google), McKinley appears to be four attached buildings. With all its nooks and crannies and wings and dormers, the school looks like it would be a spelunker's dream.

On the other end of the spectrum is the fetching Fifteenth District No. 2, a few blocks away at 1312 North Twenty-seventh Street. This wonderful building is in beautiful shape. Built in 1893, I initially speculated that it was designed by Gerrit DeGelleke, who was architect for the school board from

1905 to 1918 and also did work during other periods (including Juneau High School in 1931) with his firm Van Ryn & DeGelleke.

While the building would fit in alongside Eschweiler's buildings on the University of Wisconsin–Milwaukee (UWM) campus that were built at the turn of the century—like Johnson and Holton Halls, for example—look at neighboring Sabin Hall on the UWM campus to see the kind of work Van Ryn & DeGelleke were doing in the 1920s. However, John Linn, manager of design and construction at the district, said that the architects were George C. Ehlers, with Charles E. Malig, associate, who did other MPS projects, including Auer Avenue and Siefert Schools and an addition to Alexander Mitchell.

There is an addition on the south side that appears to have been added in the 1960s—grafted onto an earlier, somewhat more harmonious addition—but I'm not going to let that ruin my opinion of this building (even if it does destroy the view of the building from the south).

In recent years, the building housed the Urban Waldorf School before reverting to Twenty-seventh Street School and, finally, closing a few years ago. When its doors opened again in 2011 to house the two merged Kilmer schools (one had been located on the south side, the other in the lower level of French Immersion), it was renamed James Groppi High School, in honor of Milwaukee's controversial cleric and civil rights leader.

TWINS, TRIPLETS AND EVEN QUADRUPLETS IN VINTAGE MILWAUKEE SCHOOLHOUSES

In my nosing around into Milwaukee's vintage school buildings, I found a few sets of twins—almost always fraternal, though perhaps identical in one case—and even sets of triplets and quadruplets among Cream City schoolhouses.

Considering just how many schools were erected in the last two decades of the nineteenth and the first part of the twentieth centuries, it should perhaps be expected that some designs would be used more than once, especially when the city's financial woes in the second half of the 1890s are also considered.

One set of twins is Fourth Street School (Golda Meir) and Kagel School in Walker's Point. I discussed that connection earlier. These schools are very nearly identical. Another set of twins was Fifth Street and Walnut Street—both from the pen of architect Hugo Schnetzky—though only the former is still standing. Walnut Street was built in 1888. It had ten classrooms and a third-floor assembly hall (many vintage schools have these and use them as gyms and auditoriums) and was built at a cost of $38,880 for the structure and the land at 2318 West Walnut Street.

Fifth Street, built the same year, is very, very similar. There are some minor modifications in the window configuration, and the main wing extended further, allowing for sixteen total classrooms and the third-floor assembly. The price tag for this bigger building and the land at 2770 North Fifth Street was $110,150. If not for the extension and the minor window discrepancy, these

The now-vacant Fifth Street has survived and was most recently home to Isaac Coggs School, which closed in 2007. The building was handed over to the city, and for a few years, the white painted structure housed the MLK Heritage Health Center, which has a new home two blocks away. Fifth Street has since been returned to the MPS portfolio and is currently vacant.

Like its near-twin Fifth Street School, Walnut Street School—which was located on Twenty-third and Walnut—was designed by Hugo Schnetzky. It was destroyed by fire in 1978 and subsequently razed, and a number of homes have been built on the land.

buildings would appear to be nearly identical. By the late 1920s, Walnut Street had an enrollment of 494, while Fifth Street had 726 students.

The now vacant Fifth Street has survived and was most recently home to the Isaac Coggs School, although it was closed in 2007. The building was handed over to the city, and for a few years, the white painted structure housed the MLK Heritage Health Center, which has a new home two blocks away. Fifth Street has since been returned to the MPS portfolio and is currently vacant.

Walnut Street did not enjoy the same longevity. It was lost to fire on July 25, 1978. Arson was the suspected cause. "It's definitely a suspicious fire," Acting Assistant Fire Chief Richard Seelen told reporters at the scene. Fifth Battalion chief Florian Sobczak said, "She was extremely hot. When it burns as fast as this one did, it's been going a while and usually something highly flammable has been used." Sobczak added that there were separate fires in the basement and on the second floor.

Walnut Street had been closed for about a year when the fire occurred, and the district was planning to declare the building surplus and hoped to come to an agreement to sell the building to Veledis and Lorraine Carter, who wanted to move their day-care center there. Instead, the Carters purchased the vacant McKinley School from MPS in 1985 and opened there, at 2001 West Vliet Street.

Certainly, there were other twins among vintage buildings, and as we move forward in time, we find that in the 1920s Roosevelt and Peckham junior high schools were built off the same plans, with some modifications. At the high school level, King and Pulaski—both designed by MPS architect Guy Wiley—are very similar, too.

The first instance of quadruplets that I've found is unusual in that three of the buildings are clearly triplets—Auer, Siefert and Thirty-seventh Street Schools, which were all built in 1902–3—and a fourth is pretty darn close even though it had been erected a few years earlier. That eldest sibling, Brown Street, was built in 1898 by Henry P. Mollerus and Henry G. Lotter, while George Ehlers was the architect of Siefert and Auer Avenue Schools. Is it possible that Ehlers altered their design in creating Siefert and Auer?

Curious, too, is the fact that George Birnbach is credited with designing Thirty-seventh Street School, considering that it is basically identical to Ehlers's plans for Auer and Siefert. Thinking that perhaps the two (or even all of them) worked in the same practice, I consulted city directories, which listed different office locations for Birnbach, Ehlers and Mollerus & Lotter.

Auer Avenue School on Twenty-third Street, built on roughly the same plans as Brown Street, Siefert and Thirty-seventh Street Schools, had this unfortunately situated expansion added directly in front of the façade in 1966.

According to John Linn, Milwaukee Public Schools manager of design and construction, it's not likely that they worked off the same plans, but it is possible. "They may have given a set of plans for a school to another firm and had them modify and update as necessary to match, but that is usually frowned upon—and typically illegal—although we have our contract set up that we control the copyrights on the design work," he said.

However, other architects I asked noted some precedent for architects working off similar plans, and one pointed to the example of New York brownstones. Vintage photographs at the Milwaukee County Historical Society reveal some earlier examples of twins among Milwaukee's public schools, too. Henry Koch used nearly identical plans for the Fourteenth District School (Eighteenth Street) and the First Ward School on Cass and Kewaunee Streets on the East Side.

And the Eighth Ward (on Mineral and Seventh Avenue/Twelfth Street) and Ninth Ward (Fourteenth and Galena Streets) Schools—predecessors to the current buildings on those sites, Kagel and Siefert Schools—were also twins, except for a few differing details.

The four buildings—Auer, Brown, Siefert and Thirty-seventh Street—are all built on U-shaped plans and have façades based on a central section with tall arched windows. That section is flanked by symmetrical wings, with bays of rectangular windows. Brown has five bays of windows in all three sections. Siefert, meanwhile, has seven in the central portion and three in each wing. Thirty-seventh Street and Auer are hybrids, with five in the central segment and three in each wing.

While Siefert and Brown have a pair of low dormers atop the central segments, Thirty-seventh Street and Auer do not. There is more variation, too. Only Brown adds similar dormers atop its flanks, too. Siefert and Brown also have the same dormers on the sides of the wings, directly above the side entrances. Thirty-seventh does not have these.

Brown and Thirty-seventh Street still have decorative cold-air intake vents, often mistaken for bell towers; Auer and Siefert do not. And interestingly, the entrance is positioned differently in the façades. Siefert's is centered, Thirty-seventh Street's is shifted to the left side of the main section and those at Auer and Brown are right of center. Auer is the only one of the four that has a

Thirty-seventh Street School, on Roberts Street just south of Lisbon Avenue, is now closed. It is one of a family of similar buildings that includes Brown Street, Siefert and Auer Avenue. Thirty-seventh Street was closed when MPS opened Bethune Academy nearby.

quirky semicircular section protruding from the façade. Interestingly, it spans only the first and second floors of the three-story building.

Thirty-seventh Street was smaller than Siefert when they were constructed in 1903, but the former's wings were extended to add six more classrooms in 1911. Siefert, Auer and Brown additions were put on later, too, but unlike those at Thirty-seventh Street, they are immediately obvious. Alas, because Auer backs up to the street, the only place to stick an addition in 1966 was directly in front of the building. The result is that most of the façade has since been obscured.

Auer, Siefert and Brown are currently operating as schools, but Thirty-seventh was closed in 2005. After it was shuttered, there was talk of tearing down Thirty-seventh School to build housing to replace the housing a block to the southeast that was razed to make room for Bethune Academy, which was a replacement for Thirty-seventh.

Incidentally, the 1902 Clarke Street School—the work of Henry Lotter—has a winged façade similar to those of these schools, though there are

Architect Henry Lotter, who drew Brown Street School with his partner Henry Mollerus, designed Clarke Street School (at Twenty-eighth Street) and a similar building for Fratney Street School in Riverwest in 1902.

differently arched windows. There are, however, arched brick details that echo the Siefert and Thirty-seventh façades, and it has the same low dormers as Siefert and Brown. It is also built on a U-shaped plan but has another segment added, creating a deformed E-shaped footprint.

A set of triplets comes later. In the latter part of the 1920s, three nearly identical schools were erected on the West Side, Bay View and the North Side. These triplets have some half-siblings, too. Neeskara was first, built in 1926 on Hawley Road just north of Vliet Street. Fernwood, southeast of Oklahoma and Kinnickinnic in Bay View, followed in 1927, and in 1928, Townsend Street was built on Sherman Boulevard at Townsend. A number of schools from that era were built on a similar design, although with variations. Among them are Wisconsin Avenue (1921) and Sherman (1925)—both drawn by Van Ryn & DeGelleke—and, in 1931, Garden Homes, which appears to be the work of Guy Wiley.

A CLOSER LOOK AT NEESKARA

When I look at Milwaukee schools like Neeksara and Fernwood—both built in the 1920s—I'm reminded of the stately, boxy, brick school that I went to daily for seven years, from kindergarten through sixth grade.

After spending time looking at much older public school buildings in Milwaukee—ones that are generally more ornate and featured more peaks and valleys, as well as more florid decoration—Neeskara (1601 North Hawley Road) especially caught my eye. It is solid and stately, but there are some lovely details on the exterior of Neeskara—originally Nee-Ska-Ra and named for a spring that was on the site. Amid the terra-cotta tiles above the entrances, for example, are interspersed blue tiles with whales and swans and other interesting features, like open books and lamps.

Fernwood has an identical—though less decorated—entrance design that, as at Neeskara, is integrated into the upper floors with sweeping, blocky columns. Especially beautiful and, I suspect, often overlooked at Neeskara is the sleek and majestic tapered and fluted smokestack on the north side of the building.

Inside the school, there are solid terrazzo landings in the stairwells. Checkerboard tile work adds a regal touch. Although the hallways aren't especially noteworthy now (perhaps details have been removed over the years), the woodwork in the stairwells is sturdy and eye-catching.

Nee-Ska-Ra was built in 1926, the same year that MPS created its own in-house Bureau of Buildings and Grounds to design, build and maintain its properties. Though erected in 1926, the district's own history lists a principal

Neeskara, on Hawley Road, is solid and stately, and there are some lovely details on the exterior, like the terra-cotta tiles above the entrances. The school was originally called Nee-Ska-Ra and named for a spring that was on the site.

there from '24 on because, like many other schools at the time, it began life in temporary barracks on the site before a permanent building was constructed.

I haven't found figures for Neeskara, but Fernwood cost $375,000 to construct. Both were designed by MPS architect Guy Wiley, who also built Townsend Street off the same plans. The plans for Neeskara were Wiley's first for the district.

The first principal at Nee-Ska-Ra was Edwin G. Luening, who had previously been chief administrator at Weil Street, Walker Street and Maryland Avenue Schools and stayed on at Nee-Ska-Ra until 1952, when he was replaced by Annette Garnier (née Bartz), who was principal until 1961. By the time the school celebrated its fiftieth anniversary, it had had just four principals.

Some older folks may remember Neeskara as Neeskara-Binner School. The Paul Binner School of the Deaf was incorporated into MPS in 1885, and Binner was principal through 1895. In 1950, the district decided to take an inclusive approach with its deaf elementary students and moved the Binner School classes to Neeskara from Lincoln and Cass Street Schools on the East Side.

These days, Neeskara serves about 435 kids in Milwaukee's Washington Heights neighborhood.

Fernwood in Bay View, now a public Montessori school, was built off the same plans as Neeskara. These mid-1920s plans were the first that Guy E. Wiley drew as staff architect for MPS.

Townsend Street School, sandwiched between Sherman Boulevard and Fond du Lac Avenue, is another school built off the same Guy Wiley plans used to construct Neeskara and Fernwood.

TRACING THE DECADES AT MARYLAND AVENUE SCHOOL

I am intimately acquainted with Maryland Avenue School, which is in the heart of a neighborhood in which I've lived, attended university and worked across the last three decades. Though it is now dwarfed by a giant new hospital complex, Maryland Avenue, at the crossroads of two main East Side streets and sitting on something of a little butte, once towered above the neighborhood it has served for 125 years.

The original section of the current building, which replaced a much smaller brick schoolhouse on the site (a photo of the latter—erroneously dated 1900—appears in Randy Garber's *Built in Milwaukee* volume), was erected in 1887 for $25,000, and though original drawings have been lost to time, the building is the work of Henry Koch.

That part—the most northerly section (if you exclude the low 1950s gym/cafeteria)—contained four classrooms and the de rigueur "third floor assembly hall." But as we've seen, Milwaukee was growing, and the Eighteenth District was no different. By 1890, Milwaukee's population had boomed to 204,468—up from 115,587 in 1880 and 71,440 in 1870—and in 1891, the *Milwaukee Journal* reported that

> *on the opening day of the fall school-term, fifty-seven children were turned away from the Eighteenth District School on account of a lack of room. In order to accommodate the overflow, rooms will be rented and ready for occupancy by Monday next.*

In 1893, Schnetzky and Liebert's plans for a large addition to the Eighteenth District School, now called Maryland Avenue, were realized. This original drawing shows the western elevation before it was obscured by a new entrance and chimney erected in 1951 along with a new subterranean boiler room. *Photo by author.*

A resolution to build an addition of eight rooms to the school is now pending before the common council, and the citizens of the Eighteenth ward are anxious that immediate steps be taken, since it would be impossible to house all children next spring, owing to lack of suitable halls in the ward, which otherwise might be rented.

By March 1892, the school board had put out a call for plans for such an addition, and the firm of Schnetzky and Liebert—who were building a new St. Stephen's Lutheran School on South Fourth Street around the same time—won approval for their plans, which added a long, perpendicular wing to the existing building at a cost of $24,349. While the addition is three stories tall, classrooms were built only on the first and second floor.

Rooms were still being rented in early 1893 while the expansion was underway, according to newspaper reports. And with carpenters just beginning to frame the roof in February, the *Milwaukee Journal* warned that the building wouldn't be ready before September 1. Two months later, the

Though a new boiler room was added to the south wall of the 1893 addition at Maryland Avenue in the 1920s, a modern plant was installed in a large room dug beneath the playground in 1951.

same paper reported that the Eighteenth District was showing yet another increase in student attendance.

However, as the 1892–93 school year wound down, the *Journal* reported that the Maryland Avenue addition wouldn't be fully occupied come September: "The addition to the Eighteenth District school will be completed in September and two rooms will be immediately occupied. The kindergarten now quartered in rented rooms, will find a home in the new structure. There will, however, be three unoccupied rooms in the building."

This perhaps explains a discrepancy. While the call for plans asked for designs for an eight-room building, only six rooms were finished in 1893, and it seems safe to assume that the expansive third-floor attic space in the addition was intended to house more classroom space. That space remains unfinished to this day.

In 1902, a second school, Bartlett Avenue School (originally designated District 18-2 and designed by Van Ryn & DeGelleke), was erected to meet

The new stairwell and chimney tower, grafted onto the west façade as part of the new boiler facilities, is arguably the worst thing to happen to the building visually, disrupting the harmony of the façade.

In 1902, a second school, Bartlett Avenue School—originally designated District 18-2 and designed by Van Ryn & DeGelleke—was erected to meet demand in the ward.

demand in the ward. Interestingly, in the 119 years since the 1893 wing was completed, no further classroom space has been added to Maryland Avenue. In 1920, a small boiler room was attached to the south end, and two years later, new bathrooms were constructed in the basement (still the only floor with student restrooms). In the 1930s, a new fresh-air intake squared off a corner on the west elevation, where the new and old buildings meet. Two decades later, a new subterranean boiler room was excavated and constructed beneath the playground just west of the 1893 addition, along with a stairwell and chimney tower grafted onto the west façade—arguably the worst thing to happen to the building visually—disrupting the harmony of the façade. At the same time, a Richard Philipp–designed multipurpose gym/cafeteria/ auditorium—with an underground physical plant—was added to the north, obscuring the original entrance to the 1887 building.

Other smaller changes have taken place over the years, including removal of the two original peaked fresh-air intake vents (one in the old building and the other in the 1893 addition), the bricking up of classroom windows (either to create more wall space in the classrooms or to conserve energy—or both, depending on who you ask) and, more recently, the bricking up of attic windows and the lunettes in the third-floor assembly hall window panels. The assembly hall itself was converted into two classrooms, and the only remaining clues to its existence are segments of some of the

In the early 1950s, a Richard Philipp–designed multipurpose gym/cafeteria/auditorium was added to the north, obscuring the entrance to the original 1887 Maryland Avenue building designed by Henry Koch.

interior wooden arches. But fortunately, the decorative friezes and capitals and some other exterior details remain.

Inside, in the public area of the basement, you can easily spot where the 1887 building once ended and where it now snuggles up next to its 1893 counterpart; the old rusticated stone foundation clearly meets a later brick one, and breaks in that older stone foundation indicate former exterior doors or windows.

Thanks to the building engineer, I got an impromptu tour of the building's spaces that are rarely seen by anyone beyond the engineer himself. It made me feel like a spelunking kid again and gave me a new appreciation of why these potentially dangerous areas are no place for an unaccompanied child. Though we're already below grade, we can go much deeper underground than you'd expect. Go down a few steps and you can enter the ventilation area. A door opens on a small closet-like space with two doors side by side.

On the left is a door so narrow you have to turn sideways to fit through it. But keep your hands close to your sides because along the left wall of a very cramped space is an approximately four-foot whirring fan blade that draws air down a hallway and a shaft that connects to the attic. Though the ornamental caps (often mistaken for bell towers) are gone from the roof, the vents remain. On the right is a wall composed entirely of filters—changed a few times a year—through which the air passes before reaching the fan, which then blows the air up into the public spaces of the building. On the other side of the filters is the passageway to the vent shaft, called a plenum chamber.

Along the short passageway—maybe ten or twelve feet long—you've got to plant your feet to avoid being blown over by the airflow. At the end, you can gaze three stories up the shaft to the attic, seeing the original building façade and windows on the left. Two of the walls were added later, squaring off a corner of the building's exterior, to create this shaft.

Many of these old schoolhouses have giant attics. One such attic, at Vieau School in Walker's Point, was recently converted into classroom space. The one at Garfield School has two sides, separated by the ceiling of the third-

The ornate roof vents seen on many old schools were part of a system that included an interior air shaft called a plenum chamber (like this one at Maryland Avenue) and were key components for supplying fresh air to classrooms. *Photo by author.*

Because the call for plans to expand Maryland Avenue in 1893 asked for designs for an eight-room building and only six rooms were finished, it seems safe to assume that the expansive third-floor attic space in the addition was intended to house more classroom space. That space remains unfinished to this day. *Photo by author.*

floor gym. To get from one side to the other, you climb a steep wooden ladder and walk across the beams of the gym ceiling.

The attic at Maryland Avenue School is similarly large and wide open, suggesting that it was designed for expansion, and it is copiously adorned with old graffiti (Garfield, on the other hand, has only a few scrawls). Some folks have said that there's one-hundred-year-old graffiti up there, but the oldest I found dated from 1937.

Back down in the basement, you can follow a switchback set of staircases into an underground boiler room that was built in the early '50s, when the gym and cafeteria were added to the building. Descending, I wondered what to expect. Would this boiler room be pretty cramped—almost entirely filled with the huge boiler tanks—as at the apartment building I once managed?

No, what appeared before me was a really big open space, with two giant boilers—together they might fit on the back of a flatbed semi—and ceilings that must have been at least fifteen feet high. Off to the west is another large room, which once had windows and a door along the top of one wall. But

The attic at Maryland Avenue School is large and copiously adorned with old graffiti. Some folks have said that there's one-hundred-year-old graffiti up there, but the oldest I found dated from the 1930s. *Photo by author.*

those have been bricked up, too. That room is empty, and the engineer was unsure of its original purpose. He said that the by now unused openings were sealed up because they had become leaky and it was easy for little four-legged critters to make their way in during a search for shelter.

Every day, the engineer comes down to tend the boilers, and there's an alarm system that notifies him twenty-four hours a day if the boiler should shut down unexpectedly. If that happens, he's got to come to school and get it up and running again. At the end of each academic year, he must drain and thoroughly clean each boiler, a task that can take days. It's hard to believe that a few levels up, hundreds of kids concentrate on their work without the slightest knowledge of the industrial scenes below.

Back up in the basement, where there is a computer lab, bathrooms, the engineer's office (adjacent to a room that holds the school's electricity panel), an art room, a classroom and some offices, there is a small room that serves as a parent room (storage, basically, for the Parent-Teacher Organization

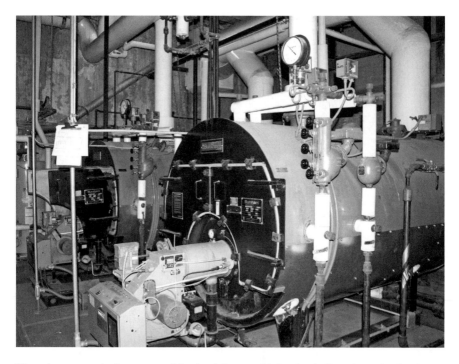

The subterranean boiler room at Maryland Avenue. It's hard to believe that a few levels up, hundreds of kids concentrate on their work without the slightest knowledge of the industrial scenes below. *Photo by author.*

supplies and event materials). It is part of a boiler room added in about 1920 that became redundant when the current boiler room was added.

Another door leads from the parent room into a room with a hardwood floor that's perhaps ten by twelve feet and is dry-walled stark white. Here are the guts of the phone system, the wireless and computer networks and the like. This is the technology hub, and it stands in bright, temperature-controlled contrast to the more workaday spaces below.

Before we go, there's one last space to check out. It is the area beneath the stage in the "new" 1950s addition. Past another heating unit, this one for water for the cafeteria and the bathrooms, is a space that's big enough to make a great classroom, which this school could really use. The problem is that it has no windows or heat and is as damp as you'd expect such a basement space to be. And who wants kids nudging themselves past a giant grumbling water heater to spend the day in a damp, dark classroom with no emergency egress?

Back upstairs in the gym that's flooded with light, I realize that I have a new appreciation not only for what it takes to keep a building like a school purring but also for the folks who do it, day in and day out, providing a safe, comfortable atmosphere in which kids can focus on learning.

High Schools Carve a
Special Place in Our Memories

D espite the fact that most of us spent roughly twice as much time in elementary school as in secondary school, we tend to identify ourselves as alumni of our high school. Maybe it's because those years are fresher in our memories, or maybe it's because those are the years in which we really begin to leap toward adulthood.

Milwaukee's early high school history was sparse. According to *Our Roots Grow Deep*, three high schools were planned in 1857 but only two were opened, and these proved to be short-lived. One of them was located in the new Edward Townsend Mix–designed Seventh District School at Jackson and Martin (State) Streets. In its December 30, 1857 edition, the *Milwaukee Sentinel* described the building as

> *the new and elegant school edifice…now about to be completed. It is a noble structure, one which our citizens may point to with pride and admiration—an evidence of educational enterprise. The building has an attractive exterior, and [is] an ornament to the city. Its furnishments within and its surroundings without are in accordance with modern improvements.*
>
> *As the opening of this school is an event worthy of note in the educational history of the city, it will not be amiss to give some general notice of the building, the school arrangements, and the advantages which the school promises to afford to the children and youth of the*

city…The ground on which it sits embraces two lots, the area of which is about 120 by 127 feet…The edifice fronts 52 feet on Jackson Street…it is 44 feet wide by 77 feet deep, height 50 feet to the top of cornice. The walls are brick, faced with Burnhams' best pressed brick. The design is in the Italian style, the façade being relieved by two towers, each 15 feet square, one of them terminating at the height of the building, the other rising 30 feet above the walls…Dressings to the windows are of cast iron, painted and sanded to imitate stone… The building is surmounted by a heavy cornice, supported by massive brackets and enriched with dentals and mouldings.

The third story of this building was home to the new high school, while lower floors housed primary- and grammar-level classrooms. Because it was beginning to be clear to Milwaukee that a grammar school education would no longer suffice in a changing world, it was the new high school that, according to the *Sentinel*, was the most worthy of celebration.

"The true idea of a Public High School," the paper noted,

is to equalize the opportunities for acquiring a thorough acquaintance with the higher branches of study; to prepare young men for the business occupations of life, or for college. It is for the want of advantages afforded in a school of this kind that many a young man, from pecuniary inability, is compelled to forego the full development of the powers of mind. A public high school in this city will bring a good education within the reach of classes, and afford equal facilities to rich and poor. Pressing onward to the same high attainments in knowledge will be found those of the most diverse outward circumstances and who may be members of families widely separate by the arbitrary distinctions of society. The high school should furnish facilities and advantages equal to those in the best academies and seminaries for acquiring a good education.

In March 1867, a law establishing a high school in the city was passed by the state legislature, and for the following decade, the city's high school had what appeared to be an ever-changing address. By the time it was about six years old, a fire drove the school to the First Baptist Church (at Ogden Avenue and Marshall Street), and it later returned to the First Ward school building on the corner of Van Buren and Juneau (then Division) Streets.

Snow covers the construction site in March 1928 at the corner of Cass and Ogden where the new Lincoln High School was being erected. In the background, the 1887 Milwaukee High School can be seen.

In 1877, Milwaukee High School settled in at the ten-year-old Milwaukee Academy building on Cass and Knapp Streets. On December 2, 1867, the *Milwaukee Sentinel* described the then new academy, constructed for $25,000, as

> *the most noticeable building in the First Ward. This is a handsome brick structure three stories in height, with a Mansard roof surmounted by a tower commanding a view of the surrounding city. It is, both externally and internally, convenient for the purposes of the Academy, and pleasing to the eye. The first story contains two department rooms, with recitation rooms adjoining, which are designed for the use of the primary and preparatory departments. On the same floor is another commodious room, designed for the use of the Young Men's Literary Society. The second story is occupied by the academic department. On this floor there is one large study room, capable of seating one hundred*

students or more, a reception room, and three recitation rooms. One of the latter will be appropriated to the use of the classes in the physical sciences, and is to be fitted up with the arrangements necessary for conducting experiments illustrative of these studies. The upper story is designed for a hall for public exercises.

A new building was erected on the southeast corner of the site in 1887. When South Division opened in the 1890s, Milwaukee High School was renamed East Side (and then, East Division) High.

By the turn of the century, high schools had begun springing up around the city. West and South Division were opened in the 1890s, followed by North Division and Boys' Tech in 1906 and Girls' Tech in 1909. Washington and Riverside were opened in 1912, and Bay View started up in barracks until its building was complete in 1922. By the start of the Second World War, Lincoln had replaced the old Milwaukee High School, and Custer, Juneau, Rufus King and Pulaski were up and running, too. The next spurt wouldn't take place until the 1960s, when Madison, Marshall and Hamilton were constructed.

To make sure that the prewar high schools get their due, here's a brief history of each.

SOUTH DIVISION. Erected in 1898–99, South was the work of Henry Koch. The school itself had opened a few years earlier and convened at what was later called Second Avenue School, at Second Avenue (now South Seventh Street) and Madison Street, from 1893 to 1899, before moving into its new building. As the city grew, the new South building seemed to shrink, and an addition, including a gym, was constructed in 1932.

South's four-story domed tower was nothing short of a neighborhood landmark on the near south side of the city for decades, so much so that when the school was demolished, shortly after a replacement was built nearby in 1977, the dome was preserved.

The original building had been added to in 1911, 1916 and 1951. But it still couldn't keep pace with the times. The district's 1969 report, "A Six-Year School Building and Sites Program, 1970–1975," made replacing South Division its top recommendation for MPS high schools. "Facilities in the various subject fields are in need of improvements to meet today's standards," the report noted. "It does not appear to be advisable to continue remodeling the present South Division building or to construct an addition on the present site."

Henry Koch's South Division High School on Lapham Boulevard would quickly become a south side Milwaukee icon. The beloved tower has been preserved and forms part of Bluemel's Garden Center on Loomis Road.

While older residents of the area—and school alumni—still mourn the loss of the "Old South Division," the dome lives on. Bluemel's Florist & Garden Service made the thirty-foot dome part of its building at 4930 West Loomis Road. Owner Mike Bluemel—whose mother, like the author's, attended South Division—purchased the dome at an estate sale auction from the antiques dealer who bought it when the school was demolished.

WEST DIVISION. West Division started out in 1895 as West Side High, holding classes in the Plankinton Library Block building on Wisconsin (then Grand) Avenue. The school's permanent home was built in 1899 on Highland Avenue (then Prairie Street), between Twenty-second and Twenty-third Streets.

The Neoclassical building was designed by Schnetzky and Liebert at a projected cost of $80,000. Milwaukee architectural historian H. Russell Zimmerman wrote of the building, "In Liebert's handsome, but restrained, composition we can once again see the influence of [Karl Friedrich] Schinkel's work in Berlin. The school sat on a rock-faced stone foundation, the first floor was in brick with banded rustification and the remaining floors were framed with pilasters supporting a frieze with triglyphs and block modillions. The projecting entrance pavilion was adorned with Greek acroteria."

The Neoclassical West Division High School building was designed by Schnetzky and Liebert at a projected cost of $80,000. Milwaukee architectural historian H. Russell Zimmerman wrote of the building, "In Liebert's handsome, but restrained, composition we can once again see the influence of [Karl Friedrich] Schinkel's work in Berlin." The building was demolished in 1951 and replaced.

Zimmerman also pointed to an unspecified contemporary newspaper report that celebrated the structure, noting, "It is not a fancy building, nor is it plain. There is no great amount of gingerbread work, but the harmony of the lines and angles relieve it from plainness and make it a work of architectural art."

Despite a 1916 addition, the building was further enlarged by the late 1920s due to its being "considerably overcrowded," according to an MPS report. The latter addition added a cafeteria, an additional gym, locker rooms, toilets and an assembly hall stage.

The building that had been attended by a young Spencer Tracy and Douglas MacArthur was demolished in 1951, and a replacement was completed in 1958. Three years later, an athletic field was constructed. In 1984, the school was renamed Milwaukee High School of the Arts.

NORTH DIVISION. North was constructed in 1907 and quickly filled up. Within a decade, despite having lost some enrollment to the new Riverside, it was the largest high school in the district with more than one thousand students. The building got a ten-room addition in 1911, and another expansion—including a library, an additional gym, twelve classrooms, a study hall and a cafeteria—was built at the end of the 1920s. Like South, North was eyed for replacement already in MPS's 1969 facilities report.

With a new building already under construction next door, there was talk of closing the school in 1976 after a fire caused damage that estimates said would have cost nearly $500,000 to repair. Due to struggles to integrate the building, some even suggested halting construction on the new building, which they felt could never be successfully integrated.

But construction went ahead, and the new North opened in 1978. A quarter century later, North was closed and replaced in the building by a number of small charter schools. However, North was rekindled and is now again occupying the building on Twelfth and Center Streets.

North Division, built in 1907, quickly filled up, and within a decade, it was the largest high school in the district, with more than one thousand students. The building got a ten-room addition in 1911, and another expansion, including a library, an additional gym, twelve classrooms, a study hall and a cafeteria, was built at the end of the 1920s.

North was already being eyed for replacement in MPS's 1969 facilities report. With a new building already under construction next door, there was talk of closing the school in 1976 after a fire caused damage that estimates said would have cost nearly $500,000 to repair. Due to struggles to integrate the building, some even suggested halting construction on the new building, which they felt could never be successfully integrated. But construction went ahead, and the new North opened in 1978.

Among the school's most famous alumni are politicians of all kinds: Golda Meir, Gwen Moore, Martin Schreiber, Annette Polly Williams and Vel Phillips.

BOYS' TRADE AND TECHNICAL SCHOOL. Tech was born in 1906 when it was opened by the Merchants' and Manufacturers' Association as the private Milwaukee School of Trades. According to a booklet touting Tech, "A year and a half later, however, the Wisconsin legislature provided a special tax levy for any city which wished to establish or take over a trade school, and the school became the Milwaukee Public School of Trades for Boys." In 1917, the school offered a six-year program (grades seven through twelve), but it became a traditional four-year high school by the mid-1930s. Tech was an all-boys school until the mid-1970s, when the name was changed to Milwaukee Trade and Technical High School.

After a 1909 fire, a new building was constructed, with new wings completed in 1911, 1912 and 1914. A number of additions were built over the years, most notably in 1929, 1958 and 1965, and Henry Koch's neighboring Park Street School served as an annex for many years. The current building, which

Another of the seemingly endless additions to Boys' Trade and Technical School in Walker's Point is underway in this 1929 photo. Look closely and you can see a group of children gathered near the entrance to neighboring Park Street School (drawn by Henry Koch), which served as an annex to Tech for many years.

Tech was an all-boys school until the mid-1970s, when the name was changed to Milwaukee Trade and Technical High School. This 1920s photo offers a glimpse into the school's machine shop.

looks unlike any other in the city, was erected in 2002, and the old building just to the north was demolished four years later.

Tech is now officially called the Lynde and Harry Bradley Technology and Trade School in recognition of a major donation made by Jane Pettit.

RIVERSIDE. Milwaukee architectural historian H. Russell Zimmerman called Riverside, designed by Van Ryn & DeGelleke, "one of Milwaukee's finest English Renaissance school buildings," describing it as an "imposing structure…reminiscent of the Elizabethan 'H' plan manor houses." The school, which had been called East Division when it was located on Knapp Street, was renamed Riverside in 1911, before construction even began.

Interestingly, at the same meeting the school board appointed Van Ryn and DeGelleke as school district architects, the board also discussed the placement of the building on the East Side site. Earlier in 1912, the Statutory Committee on School Sites and Plans reported disagreement on which direction Riverside (which would open in 1915) should face.

Milwaukee architectural historian H. Russell Zimmerman called Riverside, designed by Van Ryn & DeGelleke, "one of Milwaukee's finest English Renaissance school buildings," describing it as an "imposing structure…reminiscent of the Elizabethan 'H' plan manor houses." This photo was taken in 1915, the year the school opened.

Called East Division when it was located on Knapp Street, this school was renamed Riverside in 1911, before construction even began.

At the May meeting, the records—found in Rolland Callaway's "The Milwaukee Public Schools: A Chronological History, 1836–1986," show that, according to Callaway, "there was continuing debate concerning the proper positioning of the new Riverside High School. The Milwaukee Art Commission had submitted a proposal that the school be placed on the eastern half of the property facing east. 'In view of the fact that the park, which is an extension of a splendid boulevard, would be everlastingly ruined if the rear end of the building with its tall chimney and boiler room, be turned to the south and also because the building will always be readily seen from Oakland Avenue.'"

Of course, we know this advice was not heeded, and the building turns its back on the Frederick Law Olmsted–designed Riverside Park and Newberry Boulevard. For the record, Zimmerman noted in his *Heritage Guidebook* that Riverside is "well-sited." Executed in red brick and cut limestone, Riverside's façade, with Gothic and Tudor elements, is quite striking, especially its ornamented main entrance.

In 1912, the Statutory Committee on School Sites and Plans reported disagreement on which direction Riverside (shown under construction here) should face. The building faces Locust Street, turning its back on the Frederick Law Olmsted–designed Riverside Park.

WASHINGTON. The Van Ryn & DeGelleke firm followed Riverside with another English Tudor–style high school, this time on the still wide-open but rapidly expanding northwest side. In 1912, the Statutory Committee on School Sites and Plans gave the go-ahead to seek, in Callaway's words, a "suitable site in the Twenty-Second Ward with North Avenue on the north, Vine Street on the south, Forty-Eighth Street on the east, and Fifty-Second Street on the west. There was great concern at this time about the need to speed up construction, including a suggestion to offer a prize for a design." That prize, however, was likely not required since Van Ryn and DeGelleke were appointed school architects the same year.

Zimmerman, who was apparently a big fan of this style of architecture, raved about the building: "Light tan scratch-face brick, the building is set on a limestone ashlar foundation and is trimmed with cut and carved

Washington High School, the auditorium of which is seen under construction here, recently celebrated its centennial. Located on the west side, Washington has one of the most prestigious lists of alumni among city schools, including Senator Herb Kohl, baseball commissioner Bud Selig, NBA star Latrell Sprewell, Wisconsin governor Lee Dreyfus and actor Gene Wilder, among others.

Van Ryn & DeGelleke followed Riverside with Washington, another English Tudor–style high school, this time on the still wide-open but rapidly expanding northwest side.

stone. The entrance pavilion, with its battlemented parapet and random quoins, is decorated with richly carved panels and corbels."

By 1927, enrollment at Washington was a whopping 2,300. Compare that to 1,450 students at Riverside that year. The building was expanded to the north in 1971. For a time, nearby Thirty-eighth Street School served as a Washington High annex.

The school, which recently celebrated its centennial, has one of the most prestigious lists of alumni among city schools, counting among them Senator Herb Kohl, baseball commissioner Bud Selig, NBA star Latrell Sprewell, Wisconsin governor Lee Dreyfus and actor Gene Wilder, among others.

GIRLS' TRADE AND TECHNICAL SCHOOL. The main portion of the former Girls' Tech, now the Milwaukee Rescue Mission on Eighteenth and Wells Streets, was designed by respected hometown architect Edward Townsend

A neighborhood pooch watches as a 1916 addition is constructed at Girls' Trade School on Eighteenth and Wells Streets. The original building was built in 1885 by Edward Townsend Mix to house the State Normal School. Henry Koch's Eighteenth Street School can be seen in the background behind a series of barracks classrooms.

Mix and erected in 1885 to house the state Normal School. It is a graceful Queen Anne–inspired structure with three central triangular gables.

The first of a number of additions followed in 1898. Nine years later, the city purchased the building, and the trade school was opened with the support of Lizzie Kander, author of *The Settlement Cookbook*.

In 1924, the school became the fully accredited four-year Girls' Trade and Technical School. MPS put up two more additions in 1917 and 1932, and an auditorium was built in 1948. Four years later, the school ceased accepting incoming students, and in 1955 it closed. The following year, it became Wells Street Junior High. In 1978, the school closed, and five years later, the building was purchased by the Milwaukee Rescue Mission, which was being displaced from its Fourth Street location by the construction of the Bradley Center arena.

BAY VIEW. As was common in the early part of the twentieth century, Bay View High School began life in 1914 in barracks, temporary buildings that were also sometimes called relocatables and demountable classrooms. A 1917 photo shows the barracks, erected on the site of the current football field. Beyond, nearby Dover Street School is easily recognized.

As was common in the early part of the twentieth century, Bay View High School began life in 1914 in barracks, temporary buildings that were also sometimes called relocatables or demountable classrooms. This 1917 photo shows the barracks, erected on the site of the current football field. Beyond, nearby Dover Street School is easily recognized.

Bay View finally got its own permanent building in 1922, a stately English Tudor Revival structure—like Riverside and Washington, the work of Van Ryn & De Gelleke—topped with gargoyles.

Bay View finally got its own permanent building, a stately English Tudor Revival structure (again the work of Van Ryn & DeGelleke) topped with gargoyles, in 1922. In photos of construction of the building, the site is bounded by fields. But those meadows soon succumbed to subdivision, except for the adjacent Humboldt Park, and although Bay View High opened with an enrollment of 850 in 1922, just five years later there were 1,600 pupils.

But it would be a long time before the teachers and students would get some elbow room. In 1958, the study hall was converted to seven classrooms. An addition to the north end of the building, including a 1,200-seat gym, was opened in 1976. Currently, the Bay View High building also houses the former Fritsche Middle School program.

LINCOLN. I discussed Lincoln's history a bit in the first chapter and at the start of this one, so here I'll add just a few more details. The first public high school was opened on the site when Milwaukee High School moved into the then twelve-year-old Milwaukee Academy building on Cass and Knapp Streets. A new school opened on the site in 1887, and it was rechristened East Division High School when South and West Division were completed in the 1890s. East Division got a new home on the upper East Side in 1915 and was renamed Riverside. The building housed a deaf school for a short time, and in the fall of 1920, Lincoln was reopened, first as a junior high school and later expanding to a six-year high school, quickly testing the limits of the old building.

Guy Wiley designed a new building, estimated to cost $1.25 million, that was completed on the north end of the block (while the previous building still stood on the south side of the lot) in 1928. That building still stands today, though the high school program was closed in the spring of 1978, and is home to Lincoln Middle School of the Arts.

Among Lincoln's alumni are Oprah Winfrey, singer Al Jarreau, novelist Robert Bloch and NBA all-star "Downtown" Fred Brown.

Guy Wiley designed a new Lincoln High building, estimated to cost $1.25 million, that was completed in 1928. That building still stands today, though the high school program was closed in spring 1978, and it is currently home to Lincoln Middle School of the Arts.

Built in 1924 as North Milwaukee High School, Custer came into the district as a six-year school (grades seven through twelve) in 1930 after North Milwaukee was annexed by the City of Milwaukee in 1929.

CUSTER. Built in 1924 as North Milwaukee High School, Custer came into the district in 1930 after North Milwaukee was annexed by the City of Milwaukee in 1929. It was a six-year school. It began as a considerably smaller school than its counterparts, with an enrollment of 651 in 1930 that grew to 793 in 1931 and 957 in 1932. A replacement building for Custer was erected in 1955.

SOLOMON JUNEAU. One of three handsome moderne (or Art Deco) style Milwaukee public high schools, sources attribute the plans for Juneau to Gerrit DeGelleke, who along with his firm Van Ryn & DeGelleke did much MPS work, though typically during an earlier period. It's surprising, too, since Guy Wiley was already MPS's staff architect by the time Juneau was erected in 1931–32, and it looks very similar in style to Wiley's Rufus King and Casimir Pulaski High Schools built in the following years.

The three-story steel-frame Juneau building was constructed with a light brick façade with large windows, mostly in glass block but with a band of squat windows along the bottom of each opening. A decorative frieze runs along the roofline, and ironwork with swirls and grid patterns adorns the entrances.

An addition was built to the south in 1976, and despite a good match on the brickwork, the new building lacks the details (such as the frieze) of its elder sibling.

One of three handsome moderne/Art Deco–style Milwaukee public high schools, sources attribute the plans for Juneau to Gerrit DeGelleke, who, along with his firm Van Ryn & DeGelleke, did much MPS work, though typically during an earlier period.

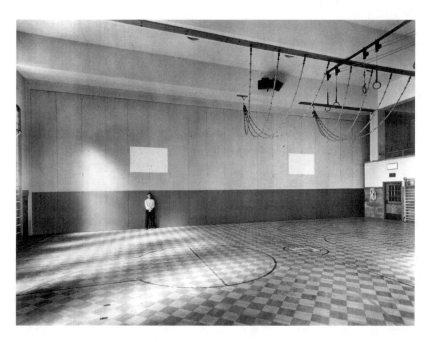

An addition was built on the south end of Juneau in 1976, and despite a good match on the brickwork, the new building lacks the details (such as the frieze) of its elder sibling. This photo shows the original building's gym.

Juneau, which was, for a time, a six-year high school—grades seven through twelve—closed in 2005, though it has since reopened as a home to charter schools Montessori High School and Community High School. MacDowell Montessori moves into the building for September 2012 and will expand to a public K3-12 Montessori program.

RUFUS KING. In its 1929 report, "A Five Year Building and Future Sites Program," MPS reported in a section on junior high schools that "a site for another school within the city limits at Seventeenth and Olive Streets has also been purchased," which reminds us that Rufus King was originally planned as a six-year high school, encompassing grades seven through twelve.

MPS architect Guy Wiley designed the Art Deco structure, which was begun in 1932 and completed in 1934 at a cost of $1.3 million. It had a pleasing set-back design mimicking outstretched arms, with an impressive central tower, and the plans would later be tinkered for the construction of Casimir Pulaski on the city's south side.

MPS architect Guy Wiley designed the Art Deco Rufus King High School, begun in 1932 and completed in 1934 at a cost of $1.3 million.

According to the school's own history, which notes that the school is a product of the Works Progress Administration, "The designs and execution of the building's plaster work, stone work, woodwork and other details were supplied by local artists and craftspeople. The art deco style…makes Rufus King a special gem among its modern, stark, spartan peers."

According to the school's own history, which notes that the school is a product of the Works Progress Administration, "The designs and execution of the building's plaster work, stone work, woodwork and other details were supplied by local artists and craftspeople. The art deco style...makes Rufus King a special gem among its modern, stark, spartan peers."

Despite the six-year school plan, King opened as a traditional four-year school with an enrollment of 1,225. A 15,000-seat stadium was also erected on the twelve-acre site. The building was expanded in 1999.

CASIMIR PULASKI. According to a newspaper report, "the first shovel of dirt was turned" in the construction of Pulaski on December 22, 1937. The building— which the paper claimed was "by far the largest of the 22 new schools and additions that Guy E. Wiley, school board architect for 15 years, has designed"— was completed rapidly, in just under eighteen months.

That wouldn't have seemed long for a school that had spent six years inhabiting barracks (the fourteen initial barracks grew to forty), put up to alleviate overcrowding at South Division and Bay View, while awaiting a permanent home. Some of that time was passed as what the newspaper

Pulaski High School, a larger sibling to Guy Wiley's earlier Rufus King High School building, was completed rapidly, in just under eighteen months.

The new Pulaski building included an impressive library, seen here. The building was much needed to replace dozens of barracks erected to house the popular school for as long as six years.

Pulaski High School's new home came after the academic program had spent six years in the temporary barracks shown here. Initially, there were fourteen such temporary structures at Pulaski, but that number had grown to forty by the time the building was completed.

called "storms" raged over the cost of the new building, which was designed on the plans of Rufus King but was 25 percent larger than King.

"It is generally accepted now," the *Journal* wrote, "that the reason Pulaski cost so much [$2.4 million] was because it is such a large project and because its contracts were awarded at a time when the labor and building material markets were rising—not because it is so elaborate or ornate."

BAY VIEW FEARED CLOSURE
OF MOUND STREET SCHOOL

I t's interesting the way that a myth can grow and trickle down through the generations. Consider the story that aged along with the former Mound Street School (2148 South Mound Street) in Bay View.

Opened in 1886 as District 12-2, a companion to District 12-1 (later called Allen School), the school—designed by Walter Holbrook, with an addition by Van Ryn & DeGelleke—was renamed for its location in 1912, when many other schools were similarly rechristened.

Barely twenty years earlier, the street was planned by Edward Allis (of Allis-Chalmers) and future mayor Ammi R. Butler and named Mound Street in honor of the Indian mounds located on Sixth and Lincoln nearly a mile away.

By 1974, an MPS history noted that the street crossed an Indian mound, leading to the name. Four years later, when the school was tagged for closure by the district, a newspaper article claimed that "the school was built in 1886 over an ancient Indian burial mound." In his book *Milwaukee Streets: The Stories Behind Their Names*, Carl Baehr debunked the enduring falsehood: "The small hill this street runs over is not one of [the mounds], as street lore has claimed."

What is not myth is the deep meaning and value a school can embody in a neighborhood. Sometimes that value is felt more in the heart than in real estate values, however. "Because the school is closing, residents fear there will be no incentive for young families to move into the area," wrote reporter Douglas Rossi in the *Milwaukee Journal* in October 1978. "If no young people

Bay View's Mound Street School opened in 1886 as District 12-2. The building was designed by Walter Holbrook, with an addition by Van Ryn & DeGelleke.

move in, some fear the neighborhood will turn into a slum. The proliferation of 'For Sale' signs on houses in the area is fueling their concern."

Fast-forward three decades, and Bay View is one of the city's hottest neighborhoods—and still popular with families. Discussions have come full circle as Parents for Bay View Schools lobbies MPS to give Bay View High School a neighborhood focus to prevent families with children fleeing to the 'burbs to find suitable schools.

Then, as now, neighborhood concern about the closure of a school—in this case, Mound Street—was easy to understand. The school board suggested closing Mound Street because of declining enrollment. According to Rossi's article, the attendance area population was aging, and as Milwaukeeans know, the northern edge of Bay View, where Mound Street is located, is heavily industrial rather than residential.

Some Mound Street families had been through this before, or their grandparents had. When Jones Island School was closed in 1919 as part of the depopulation of the now entirely industrialized peninsula, many of the neighborhood children moved to Mound Street.

The latter school was erected in 1886 at a cost of $98,650 for the land and improvements. It was expanded in 1896 and modernized three years later. At that point, it boasted fourteen classrooms, a small assembly hall

In 1957, Mound Street served as a model for other MPS buildings of its vintage when a "pilot room" was added. This is a "before" photo of room 16.

The pilot room—seen here in an "after" photograph—was a remodeled classroom that was meant to serve as an illustration of how these solid old buildings could roll with the changes.

and a basement with a lunch room and bathrooms. By the late 1920s, the relatively small school had an enrollment of 626, an astonishing fact for anyone familiar with modern school enrollments.

In 1957, Mound Street served as a model for other MPS buildings of its vintage when a "pilot room" was added. The pilot room was a remodeled classroom that was meant to serve as an illustration of how these solid old buildings could roll with the changes. These new rooms were clean, sleek and efficient. Gone were the ornate moldings, wainscoting and fixtures, replaced by modern fluorescent lights running nearly the length of the room. Out with the old cast-iron and wood desks bolted to the floor, with flip-up seats attached to the desk behind; in with simple, easily moved, utilitarian chairs, two to a table.

Old, inefficient windows were replaced with modern examples with shades that rolled down to the bottom and up to the top from a scroll in the

Old, inefficient windows were replaced with modern examples with shades that rolled down to the bottom and up to the top from a scroll in the middle. Tall doorways capped with transom lights were replaced with contemporary, metal-framed doorways.

middle. Tall doorways capped with transom lights were replaced with metal-framed contemporary doorways.

Room 16 also got an acoustical ceiling, new blackboards, radiant heat and a refinished floor, though existing floors in less pristine condition were promised linoleum or asphalt tiles. Finally, the walls were painted light yellow and green.

According to a newspaper report, the room was "transformed as an experiment which will help guide the modernization of teaching quarters in many of the school system's older buildings. Modernization of older schools formed a substantial part of the program which got the go-ahead signal last spring when Milwaukee voters authorized the issue of 39 million dollars in bonds during the next five years to meet future school housing needs. Nearly six million dollars of that amount was earmarked for the improvement of serviceable schools in established areas of the city."

In order to make the most of that money, the school board decided to create a one-size-fits-all classroom that it could retrofit into old buildings. Room 16's makeover cost $5,000 for construction and $800 for furniture. Contrasting that with estimates of $30,000 to $35,000 per room for a new permanent school, the board figured that it was on to something.

But tinkering with classrooms couldn't change the reality of enrollments and their effects on school budgets. By the late 1970s, MPS was ready to close a number of schools: Liberty-MacArthur, Fifth Street, Ludington, Warnimont Avenue, McKinley, Jefferson, Mound, Wells and Clarke Street Annex.

Neighborhoods were concerned. Downtown barber Jose Ortiz had two children at Mound Street. "Close the school," he told the *Journal*, "and it will hasten the run to the suburbs. A school holds a neighborhood together. I believe in this neighborhood. I own my own home there. They talk about integrating the schools; well, we've done it. We have a multicultural neighborhood, with good, hard working people in it."

But while these days it's often hard to find a buyer for a century-old schoolhouse in a down economy, MPS had interested buyers for a number of properties. Milwaukee School of Engineering (MSOE) and a yoga school expressed interest in Jefferson (located just west of Juneau Village), a day-care operator purchased McKinley (and still owns it) and there were at least three parties interested in Fifth Street: the City Health Department wanted it for a health clinic, a church sought to open a day care there and the Opportunities Industrialization Center hoped to use it as a job training site.

Room 16 at Mound Street School also got an acoustical ceiling, new blackboards, radiant heat and a refinished floor, though existing floors in less pristine condition were promised linoleum or asphalt tiles.

Maybe Bay View did okay despite the closure of Mound Street School in the spring of 1979 because it, too, had a buyer. Towne Realty bought the building and tapped KM Development to remodel it into Winchester Village.

The building still lords over its quiet Bay View street. But instead of housing children during daylight hours, Mound Street has carpeted hallways leading to forty-eight apartments for the elderly and handicapped. Within a few months of opening in February 1983, it was at full occupancy.

Two of its first residents were sixty-seven-year-old Cecelia Wawrzyniakowski and seventy-nine-year-old Helen Sedivy. For them, moving in was something of a homecoming. "I started kindergarten here and went up to the seventh grade," Wawrzyniakowski told newspaper reporter Marilyn Gardner. Tillie, as she was known to her friends, said that she loved the school.

Sedivy's return was perhaps ironic. "I hated school," she told Gardner. "I played hooky, and there was a truancy officer right there saying, 'You get back to school, little girl.' No matter what route I took [to skip school], that son-of-a-gun was always on my tail."

POTTER'S LEGACY LIVES ON
AT GAENSLEN SCHOOL

Though Milwaukee's Gaenslen School—which currently has a special-needs population approaching 50 percent—is named for Milwaukee's first orthopedic surgeon, Dr. Frederick J. Gaenslen, an argument could be made that it should have been called Potter School.

Then MPS superintendent Milton Potter was the force behind the first classes held specifically for handicapped children in 1913. Though that program was short-lived, Potter was determined to help educate students who couldn't physically get to regular classes.

He next started a system of providing instruction in the homes of children. By 1917, MPS—with Potter still at the helm—built the Lapham Park Open Air School at Eighth and Walnut, next to Ninth Street School (currently the site of Elm Creative Arts, Alliance School and Roosevelt Middle School of the Arts). According to a district publication from a decade later, the school, which had an enrollment of 132, "provides education for weakened children in a wholesome atmosphere."

As the name implies, the building's many windows could be flung open to provide a constant stream of fresh air—such as it might have been in early twentieth-century industrial Milwaukee—which was recommended for many ailing children. Cots were provided in classrooms to, in the words of a newspaper photo caption of the day, "make children comfortable."

In 1928, the school welcomed children with physical disabilities, too. Although eleven kids were at the handicapped school on its first day,

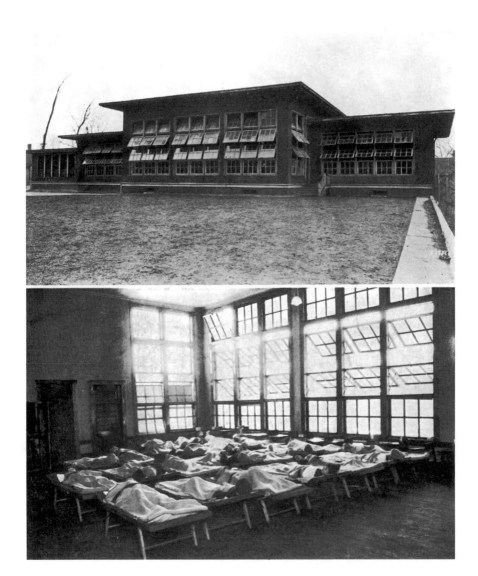

By 1917, MPS built the Lapham Park Open Air School at Eighth and Walnut, next to Ninth Street School (both razed). According to a district publication printed a decade later, the school, which had an enrollment of 132, provided "education for weakened children in a wholesome atmosphere."

In 1939, a new state-of-the-art Gaenslen School building, designed by Alexander Bauer of Eschweiler and Eschweiler Architects Associated, was erected along the Milwaukee River on a six-acre site between Burleigh Street and Auer Avenue in Riverwest.

enrollment was expected to be about twenty, and the district provided transportation for them. Nine years later, the school—which was educating kids who "needed open-air treatment" and those who were handicapped— was renamed Gaenslen.

In 1939, a new state-of-the-art building, designed by Alexander Bauer of Eschweiler and Eschweiler Architects Associated, was erected along the Milwaukee River on a six-acre site between Burleigh Street and Auer Avenue in Riverwest. The building's classroom wing overhung the riverbank, with views out across the river and the riverfront property, which had been designated as a bird sanctuary.

When the new Gaenslen building opened, it served a K-12 population, and according to a *Wisconsin Architect* article that appeared after the building's completion, there were "cases of infantile paralysis, spastic paralysis, or other birth injuries, cardiac difficulties, and accidental injuries. Anyone who anticipates a depressing sight, will be amazed at seeing these children…They are probably the most cheerful group of pupils at any school in the city."

Interestingly, Gaenslen's innovations may have helped render it outmoded at an early age. A year before the building (pictured here upon its completion) would have celebrated its fiftieth anniversary, a replacement building—the current Gaenslen School—was completed.

The February 1940 article describes the building, which was a single-story, variegated brick building with limestone trim with an Art Deco flair, as having four functions: instructional, therapeutic, recreational and administrative. "Many inquiries have already been turned over to the architects for information concerning the many unique innovations included in the design and plan of the new Gaenslen School."

Interestingly, Gaenslen's innovations may have helped render it outmoded at an early age. A year before the building would have celebrated its fiftieth anniversary, a replacement building—the current Gaenslen School—was completed.

"The old building may not have been that old compared to others in MPS's inventory of educational facilities," said Mark Zimmerman of Zimmerman Architectural Studios, which designed the current building, "but the needs and strategies had advanced [so] that the old building was not as user-friendly with where the needs and the competition across the country were for these students with special needs."

Zimmerman, whose firm has designed a number of schools, added that there were many things to consider in designing Gaenslen: "It was not a simple or typical tweak of a traditional school floor plan. Some of the drivers of the design were meeting a wide range of physically challenged students and their mode of mobility assistance, from wheelchairs, to wagons, to 'creepers,' but there was a full spectrum of mobility challenges and needs."

Because attitudes toward children with diverse needs have changed over the years, the approach to designing a school that serves those children has changed, too. There is perhaps an increased sensitivity to not only physical but also emotional needs. "You add a want and need for equity and fairness," said Zimmerman. "Able-bodied students were an important part of the student population. They wanted to achieve a mix of mainstream students learning side by side with physically and mentally challenged students. So as not to call attention to the handicap, chalkboards, for instance, were built away from the wall so the knees didn't get jammed while a student completed a math problem at the board while seated in a wheel chair."

New teaching and learning methods also affected how educators envisioned a new Gaenslen School building. "Teachers wanted flexibility to open up these fixed barriers from old, traditional schools and teach in groups and teams," recalled Zimmerman.

Couple that with added space for maneuvering and access, and the need for a new school was apparent. There were spaces programmed for therapy including hydrotherapy, indoor play areas for rainy or snowy days with floor drains allowing for messy projects [and] with hose-down clean-up capability included, covered bus dropoff areas...

In the old school, the kids were let off one by one with a motorized platform that raised and lowered students very inefficiently and slowly. On a rainy or snowy day, these kids would be out in the elements getting wet and cold waiting to load or unload. Now they're at the same level as the bus floor and covered.

So, now that the current building is half the age its predecessor was when it was demolished and replaced, will advances in technology and changes in approaches to educating special needs students mean that Gaenslen School will need to be replaced in the next couple decades?

"Tough question," said Zimmerman.

I think we [as a society] have become somewhat of a disposable society. In the late '80s, I was part of the Bradley Center design team. To hear talk of replacing it less than twenty-four years after it opened shocks me. But there is an embrace of sustainable design concepts and principles as well as environmentally responsible gestures like recycling old buildings/current buildings and finding adaptive reuses for architecture that once functioned to a different user.

One thing that was visionary in Gaenslen was the moveable classroom walls, which made the buildings and spaces adaptable, flexible and nimble. The test of time will be: was it flexible enough? I probably wouldn't recognize a classroom today from when I was in school. With laptops, iPads, smartboards and the like, the environments and the way children pay attention and learn are remarkably different.

Creating the current Gaenslen building was exciting, said Dave Stroik, Zimmerman president and CEO. "We did the school just as accessibility was becoming a hot topic, so it was fascinating to be on the bleeding edge. The new building was able to deal with many more issues of independence than the original, such as projecting chalkboards that allowed real wheelchair access and a 'stimulation' room that blasted sound and light to underdeveloped senses of some of the students."

Stroik pointed out that while it wasn't possible to save the Eschweiler and Eschweiler building, he did make sure that it lived on in some way in the new building. "We incorporated some of the original art and the nursery rhythm friezes into the new building," he said. "But it was difficult to capture all of the intimate charm of the original school."

Looking At, and Into, Trowbridge Street School

Trowbridge School of Discovery and Technology (1943 East Trowbridge Street) in Bay View has been staring me in the face for years. Living in Bay View for six years, I walked past it regularly. But I never really looked at it. I *saw* it, certainly. How could anyone miss the sea of concrete behind the school? I even looked at a house for sale directly across the street. But I never really did more than give it a passing glance.

So, it came as something of a revelation when I decided to drive down to Bay View and take photos of current and former elementary schools in the neighborhood, including this one, which was originally District 17 Primary, later designated in 1905 as District 17-2 (nearby Dover Street was District 17-1) and in 1912 as Trowbridge Street.

The school—which currently runs from K4 through eighth grade—originally housed first- through sixth-grade classes. Kids then went to Dover for seventh and eighth grades until Trowbridge was expanded to include seventh and eighth grades in 1905. Its most famous alumnus is Oscar-winning Hollywood actor Spencer Tracy.

I realized that I had let the sprawling schoolyard distract me from what might be the loveliest vintage building in MPS. Principal Tom Matthews invited me down for a tour, so I returned to see the inside, and he told me that he believes it is the only vintage Cream City brick schoolhouse that has never had a painted exterior. I've never come across another example, so I suspect he's correct. And looking at how stunning Trowbridge is, in its original paint-free state, it makes me wonder just how beautiful other old Cream City brick

Walter Holbrook's stunning Queen Anne Trowbridge Street School in Bay View is supposedly the only Cream City brick MPS building that has never had its exterior covered in paint.

schoolhouses would be after a good chemical wash (sandblasting damages the crumbly bricks).

Most of the schools burned coal for heat, and the soot was more easily painted over than sandblasted off the buildings. Somehow, this 1894 Queen Anne building, with its arched Romanesque portal and pleasing details, escaped that fate.

However, the interior of the building—designed by architect Walter A. Holbrook, who also drew the plans for McKinley Avenue and Mound Street Schools—couldn't boast the same success over the years. "When I got the building, it was somewhat in disrepair," Matthews said, noting that he's since replaced all the windows and doors and opened up the windows in the Romanesque arch above the main entrance, which had been boarded up.

Matthews said that when he took over, the main hallway was painted a sort of "Pepto Bismol pink" that can still been seen in some parts of the building, and the second floor corridor was "macho muscle car purple. I had Marquette's rugby team come in and paint the first weekend I was here because I couldn't handle it...None of the rooms had been painted in over thirty years...So we've systematically gone about a plan of continuous improvement, just aesthetically and the way the building looks." He spent a year renovating a disaster of a library, too.

But Matthews has also taken what was a struggling school with declining enrollment that was on the verge of being closed and nearly doubled the number of students—two-thirds of whom come from the Bay View area—and created partnerships with First Stage Children's Theater, the Coast Guard, the Milwaukee Symphony, the Milwaukee Metropolitan Sewerage District and other local businesses and groups. The student body is roughly one-third African American, one-third Latino and one-third white, making it among the most diverse schools in the district.

Walking through the building, the hallways are empty and quiet and the classrooms orderly but lively with learning, and Matthews clearly earns the respect of his teachers—many of whom have transferred to Trowbridge to be a part of the rebirth—and his students, who don't hesitate to ask him questions, express concerns and joke with him good-naturedly. And he appears to know the names of each and every one of his 320 kids.

Matthews said that it took some time to adjust to the new environment, but now he's completely at home with the kids at Trowbridge. "They break out of line, hug my knees and say, 'We love you, Mr. Matthews.'"

Having known Tom Matthews in a previous Milwaukee rock-and-roll life, during which we often shared a stage farther up Kinnickinnic Avenue at the Odd Rock Café, I'm thoroughly impressed by Principal Matthews, who seems the perfect balance of engaged, stern, friendly, fair and concerned.

According to a 1991 historic designation study report, Trowbridge was built in two phases. The three easternmost sections—including the main entry, as well as a classroom section on either side of it—were constructed in the first phase. In 1909, two more classroom sections were added to the western side.

The school was built in 1894—four years after Dover Street was constructed west of Kinnickinnic Avenue—to replace a much smaller school that was located on Wentworth, just south of Russell Avenue. The playground behind the building was added in the 1920s and expanded in the '70s. The top floor of the building has one of the tiny gyms so common in buildings of the era—the playground expansion must have been welcomed.

The report notes that "[t]he Trowbridge Street School is architecturally significant as a fine example of a Victorian era schoolhouse by a noted Milwaukee architect. It is historically significant for its associations with the development of the Bay View neighborhood."

Holbrook was a partner of important Milwaukee architect Edward Townsend Mix in the 1880s. Born in Sackets Harbor, New York, in 1849, Holbrook arrived in Oshkosh and then, in 1869, in Milwaukee, where he began working with Mix, rising up from his role as a draftsman to become Mix's partner in 1881.

Holbrook designed the former Sentinel building at 225 East Mason Street and a number of local residences, and he also worked on many famous local Mix projects, like the Mackie Building, the Mitchell Building and St. Paul's Episcopal Church on Knapp Street. Holbrook died riding his bicycle on State Street in 1910.

Luckily, for fans of Milwaukee history and architecture—as well as for the Trowbridge community of staff, students and families—his gorgeous schoolhouse endures.

Architectural Gems "Haunted" by Schoolhouse Echoes

The thrill of "discovery" is what made me interested in getting behind the scenes looks at some vintage Milwaukee school buildings. Peeking into the attic at one school to look at decades-old graffiti left by students made me eager for more.

So you can imagine my enthusiasm when I got in to see two historic (but currently closed) MPS buildings: Garfield Avenue School at 2215 North Fourth Street, built in 1887 and designed by Henry C. Koch, and Philipp Elementary at 4310 North Sixteenth Street, a much more recent building but one loaded with incredible details in the Rufus King neighborhood.

Philipp was built in 1932 and designed by the esteemed and celebrated Milwaukee firm of Eschweiler and Eschweiler. Alexander Eschweiler's firm designed the Hotel Metro building, the Wisconsin Gas building and the Charles Allis Art Museum building, among others. As we've seen, the firm also designed the first Gaenslen School in Riverwest.

We visited Garfield first, and it was eerie. Though it was daytime, the lights were on and we were not alone—it was an official visit, so we didn't sneak in—an empty school still echoes with the sounds of thousands of young voices. And the building is not exactly empty. There are still stacks of chairs and desks in the classrooms. Here there's an old computer; there stand a few shelves of textbooks. On an office desk, there are packages from someone's final lunch in the room. Unplugged vending machines are among the few things left in the basement teacher's lounge.

Philipp Elementary, near Rufus King High, was built in 1932 and designed by the esteemed and celebrated Milwaukee firm of Eschweiler and Eschweiler. Outside, the building is adorned with terra-cotta tiles depicting fairy tale scenes. *Photo by author.*

Faded decorations on the bulletin boards remind us that Garfield was most recently home to the private Woodson Academy, which leased the building from Milwaukee Public Schools. It almost feels like everyone went home one Friday afternoon and simply forgot to return on Monday morning.

The architectural details are interesting, though the exterior is more stunning than the interior these days. But still, there are some interesting features, like large, bright classrooms, with lots of (now painted) woodwork. Like many old schools, however, Garfield has a small gym—with a stage—on the top floor, and that makes for an interesting attic.

I'd been in exactly one old schoolhouse attic previously, and that one was entered by a typical door (no stairs) from the school's top floor. Garfield's requires one to scale a steep ladder-like staircase hidden behind a closet door. Once up there, the top half of the gym separates two attics. But tall ladders allow one to pass from one side to the other over the ceiling of the attic. I wasn't allowed. But I did peek out of the tall, slender windows, which offer a great view, and we did spy some graffiti, though not as much as I saw in the other school attic. Interestingly, a large portion of the roof boards were charred, suggesting that there was once a pretty big fire there.

Philipp—named for Wisconsin governor Emanuel L. Philipp—is a much different place, though no less "haunted." I don't mean inhabited by paranormal activity but rather by the faint echoes of the pitter-pat of tiny feet in the hallways and the chatter of young voices in the classrooms.

Philipp is an arts-and-crafts dream. Outside, the building is adorned with terra-cotta tiles depicting scenes from fairy tales: cows jumping over moons, moms and their big families outside their shoe houses, Mary and her little lamb and so on.

Inside, the office, the classrooms and the hallways are all outfitted in stunning woodwork. It's a sight to see, really. But the real jewel is the giant ground-floor kindergarten room. You can enter through the cloak room, with its rows of waist-high coat hooks—each still has a child's name written on a slip of paper. (Tippecanoe School, built in 1936 on the south side of the city, has a similar kindergarten cloak room and dark woodwork.)

Then, along the east wall of the bright, airy room, is a beautiful fireplace with a three-panel painting installed on the wall above the mantel. Farther along the wall is a truly incredible tiled fish pond set into the wall. About four feet long and maybe two feet wide, with a spigot on one end above the drain, it almost looks like a bathtub.

Upstairs, the Philipp classrooms are basically uniform, with dark woodwork and lots of windows. Each still has a globe sitting on the windowsill and a flag hanging on the wall. One has a desk, atop which lies a selection of student photos and one of the teacher, too—presumably the last students and teacher to inhabit this room.

UP IN SMOKE

THREE BUILDINGS LOST TO FIRE

The 1970s weren't especially friendly to old schoolhouses in Milwaukee. In 1973, a spectacular fire decimated Eighteenth Street School. The school, built in 1876, was the oldest in the district portfolio at the time. It had ceased operation as a school in 1967 and was being used for storage—mostly school furniture—at the time. A brutal winter storm severely hindered fire department efforts to extinguish the blaze.

Five years later, in 1978, fires also spelled the end of Walnut Street School, built in 1888 (and a twin sister of Fifth Street School, constructed the same year), and Jefferson, located downtown. Arson was suspected in the Walnut blaze, and Jefferson, erected in 1899, fell victim to faulty wiring. Considering the age and construction of these buildings—and how many of them are still in daily use—it seems remarkable that significantly more have not burned.

According to a 1940s report by then MPS architect Guy E. Wiley, the buildings put up between 1875 and 1917 were of "ordinary construction," meaning that they were "of a low fire resisting character consisting of masonry exterior walls and wood joist floor construction on wood stud or brick partition walls."

Beginning in 1919, MPS constructed buildings that were what was then called "fireproof," though by the 1940s report, Wiley was already leery of that term and preferred "fire resistive." These buildings were of reinforced concrete or steel-frame construction. But even by the dawn of the twentieth century, architects were working to create schools that *were* more resistant to fire. The new First Ward School (later called Cass Street School), just south of Brady Street, is an example. Erected in 1905 according to plans drawn by Buemming and Dick, Cass Street's construction focused on improving the "fireproof" qualities of public buildings.

"The floors throughout are steel and concrete construction," noted a September 3, 1905 article in the *Milwaukee Sentinel*. "The plaster is applied directly to the brick work, and as few moldings as possible are used in the interior, thus making it fireproof in floor and wall construction. The corridor, stairways and wardrobe floors are all finished in smoothly polished cement with a sanitary base brought up against the wall...The different floors are connected by means of two seven foot wide absolutely fireproof stairways." Fourteenth District School (Hayes) was completed shortly after Cass Street and the *Sentinel*, on November 5, 1905, declared it "absolutely fireproof" thanks to its steel and concrete construction.

So, why didn't more burn? Wiley's report points to "the care which has been taken of the old non-fireproof buildings and the general alertness to any dangerous possibilities with the resulting freedom from any major school disaster proves the value of the various contributing factors which have produced this result." While schools most likely had fires—a visit to Garfield Avenue School, for example, shows considerable charring in the attic—few buildings seem to have been entirely destroyed by flames.

The fire at Eighteenth Street School (845 North Eighteenth Street), then, was significant. First, it came during a major snowstorm that hit Milwaukee on April 8–10, 1973, and brought one foot of wet, heavy snow and wind gusts up to fifty miles per hour. Streets were closed, others were blocked by stuck vehicles and the interstate was shut down for two days.

When the first alarm rang at 1:18 p.m.—less than twenty minutes after students at the adjacent Wells Street Junior High had been sent home early because of the storm—fire trucks began what, for some, would be a long, circuitous route to the blaze. According to a newspaper report, "One engine company had to go several miles out of its way to reach the fire...because of parked and abandoned cars blocking the streets." Additionally, said Fire Chief William Stamm, snow and parked cars prevented the firefighters from gaining the necessary access to the building to fight the fire.

Ultimately, twenty-five pieces of equipment would arrive to fight the blaze in the ninety-seven-year-old building, including more than a dozen engines, six ladder trucks and more than 120 firefighters. Still, the fire raged out of

Henry Koch's celebrated Eighteenth Street School caught fire during a 1973 blizzard that brought Milwaukee to a standstill and may have helped doom the structure as firefighters struggled to arrive at the scene and then to get close to the building to battle the blaze.

control for more than three hours. The building was so badly damaged that a fire department spokesman said that there was no way to determine the cause. Everything was gone; only the walls remained.

Because Eighteenth Street—designed by Henry Koch—hadn't served as a school since MacDowell Elementary had been built a couple blocks away at Seventeenth Street and Highland Avenue, no one was inside during the fire, but some firemen were treated at the scene for smoke inhalation and minor injuries and one was treated at nearby Mount Sinai Medical Center for an eye injury and released.

There were fears that the fire would spread to the adjacent, and equally vintage, Wells Street Junior High School, which began life as the Normal School in 1885, and other nearby buildings. High winds from the storm blew smoke all around the neighborhood. Teachers from Wells Street next door stood and watched nervously at the scene, hoping the west wall of the burning building wouldn't collapse onto their cars, which were parked on the playground nearby.

Although unlicked by flame, Wells Street Junior High did suffer smoke damage, and its basement was flooded by the firefighters' water. It was expected to take a few days to dry out the furnaces, and so school there was canceled.

While fire officials were leery of speculating about the cause of the Eighteenth Street School fire, they had little hesitation, it seems, in declaring that the fire that destroyed Walnut Street School in July 1978 was due to arson. Built in 1888 on the same plans as Fifth Street School, Walnut (2318 West Walnut Street) was closed in September 1977. Unlike most other schools its age, Walnut Street was never expanded or modernized, except for a small boiler house added to the west wall of the building in 1926 and some bathroom and other small upgrades completed at the same time. In the 1969 report, "A Six-Year School Building Program, 1970–1975," Walnut Street is listed among the twenty-two elementary schools in MPS that still lacked hot lunch facilities.

In contrast, Fifth Street grew in 1908 and in 1960, and it was modernized in 1961. So, as enrollments declined and the district continued working toward desegregation, Walnut Street's future was not ensured. When it went up in smoke in a four-alarm fire less than a year later—four firefighters were injured battling the blaze—it seemed plain that arson likely played a role.

"It's definitely a suspicious fire," Acting Assistant Fire Chief Richard Seelen told the *Milwaukee Sentinel*. "The roof was burning through in spots

A mere three months after Walnut Street was lost to fire, Ferry & Clas's Jefferson Street Elementary School (1029 North Jefferson Street), in the heart of downtown, suffered a similar fate.

and then it just caved in." Fifth Battalion chief Florian Sobczak added, "She was extremely hot. That fire had to be going for some time before we got there [and it's worth noting that the firehouse was quite literally right across the street, within view of the school]. When it burns as fast as this one did, it's been going a while and usually something highly flammable has been used."

Another fire official, this time unnamed, told the morning *Sentinel*, "Some of the Fifth Battalion men were the first to arrive on the scene. They had gone up to the third floor when an explosion blew them down the stairway. They are lucky to have only escaped with minor burns and smoke inhalation. The heat was so intense that we had to use aerial ladders to soak the building with water before anyone dared go back in."

Before the fire, plans were afoot to sell Walnut Street to Veledis Carter, who hoped to move the day-care center he ran with his wife, Lorraine, to the former school. "The damage is quite extensive," said Seelen. "It's demolished, it would be a waste of money to try and do anything with it." The Carters turned their attention instead to another nearby building, the

129

former McKinley School, which they purchased in the 1980s and which is still home to Carter day care.

A mere three months after Walnut Street was lost to fire, Jefferson Street Elementary School (1029 North Jefferson Street) suffered a similar fate. A five-alarm fire was discovered just before 10:00 p.m. "Had [it] happened 12 hours earlier, we would have had a school full of kids," Assistant Fire Chief Robert J. Heindl told the *Sentinel*.

At the scene of the fire on October 10, Chief Stamm suggested arson as a possible cause, though two days later, Heindl reported that he was told by the state fire marshal's office that the defective wiring in a second-floor cabinet was the culprit—this despite the fact that MPS had modernized all the building's wiring about fifteen years earlier.

The building was condemned the day after the fire and razed soon after. The site is currently home to the Milwaukee School of Engineering soccer pitch.

While the *Sentinel* noted that schools were not required to have sprinkler systems except in stage areas, it reconfirmed what Guy Wiley reported more than thirty years earlier: Milwaukee has had a good record with regard to school fires, despite the odds.

"An insurance adjuster told me that the record of school fires in the states hasn't been good," MPS director of repairs Adrian T. Wisniewski told the *Sentinel*, "but the Milwaukee record has been exemplary."

New Uses for Old Schools

We've seen in earlier chapters some ways in which old school buildings have been given new life after the erasers were clapped for the last time. While Mound Street in Bay View was transformed into apartments, Bartlett Avenue was razed and replaced with housing. After McKinley was closed, Veledis Carter purchased it, and it remains lit as a day care center. Girls' Tech, later called Wells Street Junior High, was sold and is now home to the Milwaukee Rescue Mission. Fifth Street School, later called Isaac Coggs School, was handed over to the City of Milwaukee and used as a community health center. When that moved to a newly constructed home, the city gave the again-shuttered Fifth Street back to Milwaukee Public Schools, and it sits vacant. The empty Wisconsin Avenue School, on the corner of Twenty-seventh Street, is being eyed by the Milwaukee Police Department as an evidence and records storage facility.

Following are a few more recent examples of closed district schools finding a new purpose in a changing community.

Jackie Robinson Middle School

As MPS reached the home stretch in its facilities plan in autumn 2011—which the district conducts every ten years—Superintendent Gregory

This 1920s photograph of a "typical" classroom at Wisconsin Avenue School (now closed), at Twenty-seventh Street, suggests that some schools in the district housed fifty-five or more children. That number would be deemed untenable today. Wisconsin Avenue School is now closed, and the police department is eying it for records and evidence storage space.

Thornton and Milwaukee mayor Tom Barrett broke ground on renovations to transform the former Jackie Robinson/Peckham Middle School (3245 North Thirty-seventh Street) into apartments.

The building, which is on the National Register of Historic Places and the Wisconsin State Register, is being converted into the Sherman Park Senior Living Community with sixty-eight affordable apartments for seniors. The complex will include thirty-nine one-bedroom and twenty-nine two-bedroom apartments, ranging in size from 600 to 1,200 square feet. Rents are expected to run $499 to $694 a month. The community will also include space for on-site health and vocational training services, a sixteen-seat cinema, a community center, a business center and a fitness center.

"We look forward to beginning the transformation of a vacant building with a unique history into a new community asset that offers affordable living options for independent seniors," said Ted Matkom, Wisconsin market president of Madison-based Gorman & Company, which is developing the project. "This reborn building will play a prominent role within the Sherman Park Neighborhood and again serve the community as it once did in the past."

A few months later, news emerged that the former Fulton Junior High School (which was called Malcolm X Academy when it closed in 2007) on First and Center Streets might also become housing. Twin Cities–based nonprofit CommonBond Communities expressed interest in buying the property—which, with the playground, fills an entire city block—and converting the building into fifty-five apartments for families. Both of these conversion projects rely on federal affordable housing tax credits.

DOVER STREET SCHOOL

When the educational program at Dover Street School moved at the end of the 2011 school year to the nearby former Fritsche Middle School building it shares with the Tippecanoe program, the circa 1889 Bay View school building, designed by Edward Townsend Mix and with an 1893 addition by Walter Holbrook, became the site of a planned neighborhood arts center.

According to creative director Kellie Krawczyk, the Hive at Dover would be a community collaborative arts center. "The whole idea for an arts center began when art, music and gym were eliminated from many of our neighborhood schools," she said in a video tour of the building. "So a group of us volunteers got together and [created] a plan."

Among the highlights of the plan were nearly two dozen rooms available for rent to art-centric nonprofits and individuals; office equipment available to tenants in the building at no cost; a lounge; a library of art history and how-to art books; a donation center to collect art and craft supplies for use in the public art studios; a thrift store to sell supplies to help support the project; a public art studio where students can come and make one of several prepared art projects for free or a minimal fee; kids and adult art classes; and a performance space in the third-floor "gymnatorium."

In discussing the purchase of the building from the district, a potential model for the sale was seen in the sale of Garfield School in 2011 for one dollar to community members, who planned to turn it into a neighborhood center, according to school board director Meagan Holman, who represents the district in which Dover is located. "The superintendent asked me about the disposition of Dover, since now that it is closed, it would have to have significant updates to be available to be used as a school building again," Holman said. "I suggested that we look at selling it for community arts, and he asked if I could identify a buyer. It was then that I approached Kellie, who has always wanted to run a community art center, and she and her talented, entrepreneurial friends ran with it."

Unfortunately, neither the Dover Street nor the Garfield Avenue project appeared to get off the ground, and at the time of publication, it appeared that both proposals were dead. But both offered visions for ways to keep shuttered public schools lit as beacons of neighborhood and community activity.

LLOYD STREET AND THIRTY-SIXTH STREET SCHOOLS

Some former MPS schools continue to serve as education facilities via leases to charter schools, like Milwaukee College Prep, which recently opened new schools in Lloyd Street (1228 West Lloyd Street) and Thirty-eighth Street (2623 North Thirty-eighth Street) Schools. There has also been talk of MCP purchasing the buildings from the district, though that has not yet happened.

"It is my understanding that they are leased with an option to buy," MPS's now former media manager Phil Harris said. With the leases, MCP also opted to open the two new campuses as MPS instrumentality charters (meaning they are staffed by MPS employees), tying them more closely to the district.

While Thirty-eighth Street has been vacant, Lloyd only recently became surplus when the school board voted in the spring of 2011 to merge its program into Hopkins Street School to create Hopkins Lloyd Community School. In 2010–2011, Lloyd had an enrollment of about 440 pre-K through fifth-grade students, according to Great Schools.

When news of the leases emerged, MCP principal Robert Rauh said, there was no plan to purchase the buildings. "Right now, our focus is solely on getting the two buildings ready…fully enrolled and staffed," he said. "It's nice to have options down the road, and we will begin to consider those once the dust has settled."

Here are some facts about the school buildings:

- Lloyd Street has twenty-eight classrooms, and Thirty-eighth Street School has twenty-five classrooms and one lab.

- Lloyd has 69,553 square feet and Thirty-eighth Street 103,892 square feet of building space.

- Neither of the former MPS buildings is air conditioned.

- Lloyd Street, built in 1910, has a replacement cost of $17,131,026, and estimates put a replacement cost on Thirty-eighth Street School, built in 1911, at $25.5 million.

In addition to a presumed infusion of cash, MPS would save a fair bit on maintenance if MCP exercised its option to buy the two buildings. As part of its Master Facilities Plan report released on June 30, MPS was looking at $887,400 in maintenance costs at Lloyd Street School through 2016. Add in expected maintenance costs of another $176,100 over the following five years, as well as $4.3 million to upgrade electrical and plumbing systems and the addition of air conditioning, and the "Total Need" for the maintenance of the building is estimated at $5.4 million.

For Thirty-eighth Street School, the projected maintenance costs run even higher. Including the next decade of upkeep and the systems upgrades, the estimate is $7.5 million. But, of course, MCP knows that MPS's savings would become its expenses. So it will be interesting to see what transpires down the road.

THE STATE OF MILWAUKEE'S VINTAGE SCHOOLHOUSES

E very decade, Milwaukee Public Schools undertakes a new facilities plan to assess its holdings, enrollments, needs, wants and projected changes in enrollment based on demographic changes in Milwaukee. Fortunately for us, MPS completed a plan and issued a report in 2011; the lengthy report offers a detailed and extremely up-to-date snapshot of the buildings in the district.

The report was used by administration as the foundation for a slew of projected school closings, mergers and relocations—some of which passed the school board while many others never got off the ground—continuing a trend of closures that has mirrored a decline in student enrollment.

Since 2004, thirty-one school buildings have been closed (not counting changes at the end of the 2011–12 academic year). Among them were vintage buildings like Garfield, Robinson (Peckham) Middle School, Thirty-seventh Street, Philipp, Thirty-eighth Street, Malcolm X Academy (Fulton), Lee, Lloyd Street, Dover Street, Tippecanoe, Twenty-seventh Street School, Wisconsin Avenue and others.

But not all of those buildings remained closed for long. Some—like Juneau, Sarah Scott and Milwaukee Education Center—again house programs of various kinds (charter, traditional schools and so on). Others—like Malcolm X and Robinson —have been sold or are in the process of being sold. Still others have been leased, like North Seventy-sixth Street, Lloyd Street, Thirty-eighth Street and Morse.

Sixteen of the thirty-one buildings are currently vacant: South Eighty-eighth Street, Thirty-seventh Street, Philipp, Happy Hill, El Centro del Nino,

Milwaukee Public Schools are much different today than they were in the 1920s, when these children were eating their "daily luncheon of milk and crackers."

Fifth Street, Douglass, Edison, Malcolm X, Wisconsin Avenue, Carlton, Lee, Fletcher, Dover, Milwaukee School of Entrepreneurship, Green Bay Avenue and Wheatley.

At the moment, MPS, for which enrollment hovers at about eighty thousand, owns and maintains more than 18.1 million square feet of building area. There are 184 schools in 161 school buildings—two pre-K, 44 elementary, 61 K-8, 5 middle, 9 middle/high and 17 high school, as well as 58 support and recreational facilities.

The average age of an MPS building is sixty-six years old. Sixty-four buildings (accounting for 41.3 percent of the total) were built before 1930, and thirty-one are at least a century old. Just 5.9 percent of buildings date from the last thirty years. Just over half, 52.8 percent, were built between 1930 and 1980. In 1951, as a point of comparison, MPS's ninety-eight buildings had an average age of just thirty-seven years. The forty-seven oldest structures averaged fifty-nine years old, but the fifty-one newest were an average of just twenty-five years old. The district's housing stock has been aging.

The decline in enrollment has also led to excess capacity in the district. This is reflected in a calculation called Square Feet Per Student. The MPS facilities report points to the "15th Annual School Construction Report" by *School Planning & Management* magazine, which notes that "the national median enrollment and square feet per student for elementary schools was 700 students with 125 square feet per student; middle schools was 900 students with 142 square feet per student; and high schools was 1,600 students with 156 square feet per student."

Compare those numbers with Milwaukee, where elementary students have an average of 163 square feet each, middle schoolers get 277 (357 for pupils in combined middle and high schools) and high school students have 322 square foot apiece.

But not only are the buildings too numerous in contrast with district enrollment, their high average age also means that there's a lot of work to do to keep them maintained. For this, we look at the FCI, or Facilities Condition Index, a number that is reached by dividing the total repair cost, including site-related repair work and educational adequacy of the building, into the facility's total replacement cost. The resulting number is compared to a scale where 5 percent and below is best, 6–10 percent is good, 11–20 percent is average, 21–30 signifies below average, 31–50 percent means a building in poor condition, 51–65 percent is very poor and a score 65 and above makes the building a candidate for replacement.

Perhaps amazingly, given the age of the schools and the fact that roughly half of all schools have no air conditioning whatsoever (15 percent are completely air conditioned, and 35 percent are partially cooled), the district's portfolio has an FCI of 22.6 percent, just a couple points out of the "average" range.

For comparison, the report notes that Houston, which recently completed a ten-year, $1.5 billion building program, has an FCI of 19 percent, Miami-Dade scores 21 percent, Portland Public Schools have an FCI of 39 and Cleveland Municipal School District has an FCI of 80 (and 92 of its 120 buildings meet Ohio's own threshold for complete replacement). But in the middle of 2012, times are tough in Wisconsin, and state funding for schools has been slashed two years in a row. In a period of large layoffs and personnel cuts, building projects are often deferred or abandoned.

Because of the expansion of the Milwaukee Parental Choice Program (offering vouchers to be used at private schools) and the growth of schools charted by entities other than the elected school board, it's hard to accurately gauge where district enrollment will go. At the same time, city officials have assailed the district for holding on to so many properties rather than selling them. The city and the district have been playing

The average age of an MPS building is sixty-six years old, and many century-old buildings are still in use. However, Twenty-first Street School, seen here on Center Street, did not survive. It was replaced in 1978 with the Gwen T. Jackson Early Childhood and Elementary School.

tug of war with school buildings over the past two years. The former would like to sell buildings at a bargain rate to charter and private school operators, while the district—which many have suggested should work to compete with these other "market forces"—has held firm in its decision not to sell or lease buildings to its "competitors," which draw enrollment and funding from the district.

But the economic realities will continue to force changes. The 2011 facilities report predicted that the district would need $991.2 million to perform necessary maintenance and upgrades to 220 properties. That includes more than $120.0 million in plumbing work, nearly $250.0 million in electrical work and just over $400.0 million is mechanical repairs and upgrades. In the current economic climate and with the battles being fought among traditional public, charter and private schools for funding, the outlook would seem grim.

Hopefully, the same spirit that led nineteenth-century Milwaukee to hire the city's elite architects to create buildings that were enlightened cathedrals to the importance of learning and the value of a civic education available to all will lead Milwaukeeans of the twenty-first century to preserve our architectural treasures and, even more importantly, the public schools that helped build America.

Lost Milwaukee

Schoolhouse Treasures

Jackson/Detroit Street. Henry Koch's Neoclassical Andrew Jackson School (previously called Detroit Street School and District 3 before 1912) had an imposing Flemish-inspired tower nearly six stories high that was a beacon in the Third Ward community, which was initially settled by the Irish and later the Italians. The school survived the great Third Ward fire of 1892, and in 1915, a public natatorium was added, making it even more a locus of neighborhood activity. Though it was built in 1879 at a cost of $30,700, MPS records suggest that a school occupied the site from at least 1851. That it had become educationally inadequate was perhaps already clear by 1927, when the twenty-four-classroom building had an enrollment of 1,010 pupils. The building was demolished as part of the urban renewal, also sometimes referred to as "slum clearance," that erased entire sections of the old Third Ward in the late 1950s and early '60s.

Eighteenth Street. Also designed by Henry Koch, Eighteenth Street School was built in 1876 and had twenty classrooms and a third-floor assembly hall on three floors. It marked a new era in Milwaukee public school construction as it was better heated and ventilated than its predecessors. Its classical features made it popular in its day and reviews of the building, which stood behind Girls' Tech/Wells Street Junior High until it was destroyed by a spectacular fire during a brutal winter storm in 1973, were glowing.

Henry Koch's Neoclassical Andrew Jackson School (also known as Detroit Street School and District 3) had an imposing Flemish-inspired tower nearly six stories high that was a beacon in the Third Ward community. When this photo was taken, in about 1926, Jackson's student body was estimated to be 98 percent Italian.

JEFFERSON. Demolished after a fire caused by faulty wiring in 1978, Jefferson wasn't large. Designed by Milwaukee's Ferry & Clas—which created, among other buildings, Milwaukee's historic Central Library—the Cream City brick structure had two three-story wings and a central section, all with low-pitched roofs, that contained sixteen classrooms and a small assembly hall. Built in 1899, it was a more decorated version of the next school built by the district, Van Ryn & DeGelleke's Bartlett Avenue (in 1902), with ornate brickwork, including arches above the windows and diamond-shaped decorations in rectangular boxes. The entire roofline was adorned with dentil molding. It was most unusual for being a rare school building in the heart of downtown Milwaukee, and by the time it was razed, it was dwarfed by the neighboring Juneau Village apartment towers.

GAENSLEN. The original Gaenslen School in Riverwest, built into a bluff on the west bank of the Milwaukee River in 1939, was an Art Deco gem, with long wings projecting from a central rotunda. Designed by

Ferry & Clas's Jefferson Street School (built as the Seventh District School in 1899), replaced an Edward Townsend Mix school erected on the site in 1857. Jefferson Street was destroyed by fire in 1978 and demolished.

Lisbon Avenue School was acquired by Milwaukee Public Schools by annexation in 1907. It stood in a small triangle at the intersection of Forty-seventh Street and Lisbon and North Avenues and was used on and off until 1932, when it was closed and later demolished.

Alexander Bauer of Eschweiler and Eschweiler Architects Associated, it was a marvel of its day. But perhaps due to its specialized needs, it was doomed to a short life span. Its replacement, unfortunately, cannot boast the same charm.

LISBON AVENUE. This small school wasn't built by MPS but rather was acquired by annexation in 1907. It stood in a small triangle at the intersection of Forty-seventh Street and Lisbon and North Avenues. Eight years after the district acquired the school, it was closed when Hi-Mount School opened a few blocks away. But the area was growing so rapidly that Hi-Mount itself was soon bursting at the seams, and Lisbon had been brought back into use by 1920. It was finally closed at the end of the academic year in 1932 and was razed soon after. The two-story building, which appeared to possibly have attic rooms, too, was a small but stately schoolhouse of symmetrical design, with dual arched entrances flanking the central section and a pair of tall chimneys towering above the multisectioned, high-pitched roof. But for the lack of religious ornament, it could have almost been mistaken for a house of worship.

WEST AND SOUTH DIVISION HIGH SCHOOLS. Built at the same time, these were among Milwaukee's first enduring high schools, and their buildings—like others such as North Division, Washington and Riverside—quickly became beacons within their neighborhoods. Decades after their disappearances, these structures live on in the memories of Milwaukeeans old enough to have seen them. South's dome, figuratively and quite literally, towered over its neighborhood in a way that the sprawling 1970s replacement can't even aspire to. Meanwhile, iconic Milwaukee architects Schnetzky and Liebert, who drew the plans for Brumder's Germania Building and a number of landmark churches, created a timeless Neoclassical home for West Division that, like South and North, was replaced with a modern box that inspires little passion.

TEN MUST-SEE MILWAUKEE SCHOOLHOUSES

While many Milwaukee schoolhouses have features worth seeing—such as the tile work in the former Steuben Junior High (now French Immersion), the stained glass at Story School tucked behind Miller Brewing Company and the ornate stonework decoration above the entry at Humboldt Park School—here are a few buildings of special architectural or historical interest. Let this be a starting point for exploration rather than a beginning and end.

1. Garfield (2215 North Fourth Street), though no longer open as a school, fortunately continues to adorn the Milwaukee landscape. The building, constructed in 1887, is listed on the National Register of Historic Places, and its balanced Romanesque design (which includes Palladian elements, too, like faux columns), by landmark Milwaukee architect Henry C. Koch, is quite lovely.

2. Philipp (4310 North Sixteenth Street) was built in 1932 and designed by the esteemed and celebrated Milwaukee firm of Eschweiler and Eschweiler. Alexander Eschweiler's firm designed the Hotel Metro building, the Wisconsin Gas building and the Charles Allis Art Museum building, among others. Outside, it features terra-cotta panels depicting storybook scenes, and inside there is glorious woodwork galore, along with squirrels and bunnies peeking down from moldings and a kindergarten room with a fireplace, frescoes and a fish pond.

3. Fourth Street School/Golda Meir (1555 North Martin Luther King Drive) and Mineral Street School/Albert E. Kagel (1210 West Mineral Street) are great extant examples of schoolhouse siblings. [Sure, this one was harder because there are two schools listed, but I will try...] Although only Fourth Street School, built in 1890 and now renamed in honor of erstwhile Milwaukeean and former Israeli prime minister Golda Meir, is on the National Register of Historic Places, one could argue that its twin—originally Mineral Street School and now called Kagel in honor of a beloved longtime MPS teacher, principal and assistant superintendent— is the more untouched of the two, at least in terms of exterior views. They are the work of Henry Koch, and both are fine examples of Koch's take on Romanesque Revival, with rusticated stone foundations topped with brick piers capped with cornices and arches (their five-window configuration at the attic level is mirrored in Schnetzky and Liebert's Maryland Avenue School addition of 1893). The soaring chimneys are a trademark of the schoolhouses of the era, and the weightiness of the Romanesque features are tempered by the lightness achieved with copious windows. For reasons clearly other than aesthetic, no less than Van Ryn & DeGelleke plopped a 1915 heating plant addition right in front of the Fourth Street entrance at Golda, creating the idea that the front of the building is actually the back. It is for this reason that Kagel feels more authentic. Though I am not a fan of painted Cream City brick, the paint scheme currently on Golda Meir is a rare pleasing example.

4. Rufus King (1801 West Olive Street) and Casimir Pulaski (2500 West Oklahoma Avenue) were built from the same Guy Wiley plans in the 1930s, though with some variations. They marked yet another transformation of the Milwaukee schoolhouse. By 1920, buildings had become boxier, with flat, less ornate roofs, and in these two high schools, Wiley fully embraced the then popular moderne/Art Deco style. (Van Ryn & DeGelleke did the same with their plan for Juneau High during the same era.) On the occasion of its opening in 1939, the *Milwaukee Journal* called Pulaski "monumental," yet it is King—most likely due to its current popularity and academic success and to its siting—that is more acclaimed today. The view of the central tower from Eighteenth and Olive Streets is wonderful, and King's "arms" seem to reach out and embrace you as you arrive.

5. Vieau (823 South Fourth Street) was designed by no less than the firm of Ferry & Clas. The original building—there was a large expansion

Ferry & Clas's design for Vieau School in Walker's Point was unique among Milwaukee school buildings, with a stepped decoration on the peaks. Recently, a large portion of the attic in the old building was renovated to create a classroom space.

to the north in the first half of the twentieth century—is unique among Milwaukee school buildings, with a stepped pyramidal decoration on the peaks. Spelunkers will appreciate the tunnel built as part of the addition that runs under National Avenue to the site of Milwaukee Tech High School. Recently, a large portion of the attic in the old building was renovated with federal American Recovery Act stimulus funds to create a large classroom for Vieau's acclaimed Project Lead the Way STEM (science, technology, engineering and math) program.

6. Fifth Street (2770 North Fifth Street) was built in 1888 along with its twin, Walnut Street School, which burned down in 1978. Like Twenty-seventh Street School, the building is heavily weighted to the south, where a three-story section has high peaks. A lower segment juts out to the north. Walnut Street was nearly identical but with a shorter jutting wing and with slightly altered window configurations on the three-story segment. Both buildings, designed by Hugo Schnetzky, were outfitted with the third-floor

gymnasiums so common to Milwaukee schools of the era. While Fifth Street had been expanded and modernized over the years, Walnut Street was never significantly altered.

7. Twenty-seventh Street School (1312 North Twenty-seventh Street), now home to James Groppi High School, was built in 1893 and designed by George C. Ehlers and his associate Charles E. Malig with a symmetrical façade with the entrance in the center. These days, however, with two additions grafted onto the south end of the building—one attempting to mimic the style of the main building and the other not—and another added to the north, the building looks much different. Now the structure has an off-center entrance counterbalanced by a smaller entry closer to the north end. If you ignore the much later addition on the far southern end, the wide façade is still elegant. Four tall chimneys add height to further complement this long, low building. Alas, a sleek, high-pitched fresh-air intake has not survived above the main entrance.

8. Eighth Street (609 North Eighth Street), built in 1884, is located downtown, making it a rarity for that reason alone. However, the building—along with Kagel and Fourth Street School (now Golda Meir)—is a rare example of a Koch-era building with no mid-twentieth-century additions. It is also the oldest MPS building still serving as a district school.

9. Maryland Avenue (2418 North Maryland Avenue), which has been expanded a few times over the years, as we've already seen, is an example of a small Henry Koch project from 1887 (it shares similarities with Koch's Garfield Avenue School, erected the same year, with a gorgeously harmonious 1893 expansion by Schnetzky and Liebert. A new gym/cafeteria/auditorium, designed by Richard Philipp, was added to the north, covering what was likely the earliest main entrance, but the real tragedy is a new stairwell and chimney erected during the same era that blocks the wide, elegant western façade of the building and erased a nice curvature in the roofline. Despite all of that, it remains a fine example of a classic Milwaukee school.

10. Siefert (1457 North Fourteenth Street), formerly known as Fourteenth Street School, is the best example of the quadruplets discussed in an earlier chapter. Siefert, erected in 1903, has two additions, one old and harmonious and the other newer but low and easily ignored. Brown Street, nearby, has been heavily expanded over the years, and the more direct siblings are

"tainted." Auer Avenue's façade remains blocked by the unfortunate siting of a 1966 addition, and Thirty-seventh Street, which has been closed for a few years, is painted baby blue. Like Twenty-seventh Street School, Siefert was designed by George Ehlers, who also designed the Miramar Theater on the city's east side and, with John Moller, the B.M. Goldberg residence, a stunning Gothic mansion that was the first house built on the Olmsted-planned Newberry Boulevard and Lake Park.

Appendix

MPS Charts

These charts are from Milwaukee Public Schools' own history, *Our Roots Grow Deep*, 2nd edition, 1836–1967. They are included here because they are of considerable use not only in determining meanings behind school names in Milwaukee but also in tracking the changes in names, of which there have been many over the years. Where some information was lacking, Carl Baehr's useful and interesting book, *Milwaukee Street Names: The Stories Behind Their Names* (Milwaukee, WI: Cream City Press, 1995), was consulted for updates. The changes to school names since 1967 have been frequent and many. Following are some current updates—though by no means a complete list of changes over the past forty-five years, as one could perhaps write an entire book on the changes across the decades—with former names first, current (or most recent) names second.

Boys' Tech	Lynde & Harry Bradley Technology and Trade School
Burroughs Middle School	Community High School
Eighth Street	Project STAY
Eighty-second Street	Milwaukee German Immersion
Elm	Frances Brock Starms Early Childhood Center

Fifth Street	Isaac Coggs (closed)
Fifty-fifth Street	Milwaukee Spanish Immersion
Fourth Street	Golda Meir
Fritsche Middle School	Tippecanoe-Dover
Fulton	Malcolm X Academy (closed)
Garden Homes	Lloyd Barbee Montessori
Henry L. Palmer	Dr. George Washington Carver Academy
Hopkins Street	Hopkins Lloyd Community
Juneau, Solomon	MacDowell Montessori
Lloyd Street	Milwaukee College Prep
MacDowell	Highland Community School
Scott, Sarah	Wisconsin Conservatory of Lifelong Learning
Seventy-sixth Street	Satori Middle School
Steuben	Milwaukee French Immersion
Thirty-eighth Street	Milwaukee College Prep
Thirty-first Street	Westside Academy
Tippecanoe	Howard Avenue Montessori
Twentieth Street	Wheatley
Twenty-first Street	Gwen T. Jackson Early Learning Center
Twenty-seventh Street	James E. Groppi High School
Walker	Carmen Academy et al.
West Division	High School of the Arts
Wilbur Wright Middle School	Milwaukee School of Languages
Victor L. Berger	Dr. Martin Luther King Jr.

CURRENTLY VACANT BUILDINGS

Carleton
Dover
Thomas A. Edison Middle School
Eighty-eighth Street
Fifth Street
Fletcher, Dr. Arthur A.
Frederick Douglass
Fulton/Malcolm X
Garfield Avenue
Green Bay Avenue
Happy Hill
Lee
Phillip
Jackie Robinson Middle School (sold)
Sixty-eighth Street
Thirty-seventh Street
Thurston Woods
Daniel Webster Middle School
Phyllis Wheatley
Wisconsin Avenue

Tucked away on a side street off Lisbon Avenue, Thirty-first Street School—which now houses Westside Academy—is a gem of an old neighborhood school building, erected in 1895.

Name of School	Derivation of Name
Administration Building	replacement for old administration building

Secondary Schools

Bay View HS	Bay View, former area and city, now part of Milwaukee; descriptive name
Boys' Trade & Technical HS	descriptive name
Custer HS	original school located at North Thirty-seventh Street and West Custer Avenue, the latter reportedly named after an early North Milwaukee settler, Harvey Custer
Alexander Hamilton HS	American statesman
Solomon Juneau Jr./Sr. HS	Milwaukee's first permanent settler, first postmaster and first mayor
Rufus King HS	first president of Board of School Directors, first superintendent of schools, soldier, editor, jurist and diplomat

Lincoln Jr./Sr. HS	Abraham Lincoln, U.S. president
James Madison HS	U.S. president
John Marshall Jr./Sr. HS	American jurist; chief justice, U.S. Supreme Court
North Division HS	area designation; located on early Milwaukee's north side
Casimir Pulaski HS	Polish soldier in the American Revolution
Riverside HS	Located on the east bank of the Milwaukee River
South Division HS	Area designation; located on early Milwaukee's south side
Washington HS	George Washington, soldier, Patriot and U.S. president
West Division HS	area designation; located on early Milwaukee's west side

Junior High Schools

John Audubon Jr. HS	American ornithologist and artist
Alexander Graham Bell Jr. HS	inventor of the telephone
John Burroughs Jr. HS	American naturalist and essayist

Thomas A. Edison Jr. HS	American inventor
Gustav A. Fritsche Jr. HS	high school principal, MPS
Robert Fulton Jr. HS	American inventor and engineer
Kosciuszko Jr. HS	Thaddeus Kosciuszko, Polish Patriot and soldier in the American Revolution
Samuel Morse Jr. HS	inventor of the telegraph and portrait painter
John Muir Jr. HS	American naturalist and essayist
Peckham Jr. HS	George W. Peckham, superintendent, MPS
Roosevelt Jr. HS	Theodore Roosevelt, U.S. president and historian
Christopher Latham Sholes Jr. HS	inventor of typewriter
Steuben Jr. HS	Baron Friedrich Wilhelm von Steuben, Prussian soldier in American Revolution
Walker Jr. HS	George H. Walker, founder of Walker's Point and mayor of Milwaukee

Wells Street Jr. HS	*Daniel Wells Jr., lumberman, businessman and railroad executive
Wilbur Wright Jr. HS	co-inventor of the airplane

Elementary Schools

Louisa May Alcott	American novelist
Walter Allen	Walter Allen, assistant superintendent, MPS
Auer Avenue	*Louis Auer, local real estate dealer and public officeholder
Bartlett Avenue	*John K. Bartlett, distinguished local physician
Clara Barton	founder of American Red Cross
Victor L. Berger	Milwaukee editor and congressman
Blaine	John T. Blaine, Wisconsin governor
Brown Street	*Deacon Samuel Brown, west side pioneer
Browning	Jonathan and Amanda Brown, Milwaukee County pioneers

William George Bruce	distinguished Milwaukee citizen, editor, writer and publisher
William Cullen Bryant	American poet and editor
Luther Burbank	American horticulturist
A.E. Burdick	Tippecanoe/Town of Lake pioneer and donor of school site
Carleton	source unknown
Cass Street	*Lewis Cass, American statesman
Clark Street	*William Clarke, local physician and judge
Samuel Clemens	"Mark Twain," American humorist
Clement Avenue	*Stephen Clement, president of Milwaukee Iron Works and Great Lakes sea captain
Congress	*U.S. Congress
James Fenimore Cooper	American novelist
Craig	John Craig, sold site to school district in 1853

Jeremiah Curtin	American diplomat, scholar, novelist and linguist
Anna F. Doerfler	elementary school principal, MPS
Douglas Road	*source unknown
Dover Street	*Dover, England
Eighth Street	*
Eighty-eighth Street	*
Eighty-first Street	*
Eighty-second Street	*
Elm	*(street has been renamed Garfield Avenue)
Ralph Waldo Emerson	American poet, essayist, philosopher and lecturer
Engelburg	source unknown
Fairview	descriptive name

Fernwood	after subdivision
Eugene Field	American poet
Fifth Street	*
Fifty-fifth Street	*
Fifty-third Street	*
Forest Home Avenue	*Forest Home Cemetery, at the former southern terminus
Fourth Street	*
Benjamin Franklin	American statesman, diplomat, writer, publisher and scientist
Fratney Street	*Benjamin Fratney, local editor and educator
Frederick J. Gaenslen	distinguished local orthopedic surgeon and educator
Garden Homes	Garden Homes subdivision, early local cooperative housing project
Garfield Avenue	*James A. Garfield, U.S. president and general

Hamlin Garland	Wisconsin novelist
U.S. Grant	general and U.S. president
Grantosa Drive	*"Grantosa," combination of Granville and Wauwatosa
Green Bay Avenue	*
Greenfield	Greenfield Township
Hampton	*
Happy Hill	descriptive name
Hartford Avenue	*Hartford, Connecticut; one of four streets in the area named for East Coast cities.
Hawley	*Cyrus Hawley, early settler and landowner in area
Nathaniel Hawthorne	American novelist
Rutherford B. Hayes	U.S. president
Hi-Mount Boulevard	*

Oliver Wendell Holmes	American poet, essayist, educator and physician
Hopkins Street	*Otis B. Hopkins, early local druggist and real estate dealer
Humboldt Park	Baron Friedrich von Humboldt, German naturalist, traveler and statesman
Washington Irving	American writer and diplomat
Thomas Jefferson	*U.S. president, scientist, writer, statesman, inventor and architect
Albert E. Kagel	MPS acting superintendent, assistant superintendent, principal and teacher
Keefe Avenue	*John C. Keefe, surveyor who platted property in general area
Byron Kilbourn	founder of Kilbourntown, mayor of Milwaukee and railroad magnate
Joyce Kilmer	American poet
Robert M. LaFollette	U.S. statesman, senator and Wisconsin governor
Lancaster	*Elizabeth Street thoroughfare was renamed Lancaster in 1926; source unknown

Lee	*probably after an early settler named Lee who in 1831 brought first wagon load of trading goods to Milwaukee; Lee Street was renamed Meinecke Avenue
Liberty	source unknown
Lincoln Avenue	*Abraham Lincoln, U.S. president
Lloyd Street	*Nelson B. Lloyd owned a farm when the district was platted in 1860
Henry W. Longfellow	American poet and critic
Lowell	James Russell Lowell, American poet, essayist, editor and professor
Ludington	probably Harrison Ludington, lumberman, Milwaukee mayor and Wisconsin governor
General Douglas MacArthur	American soldier and statesman
Edward A. MacDowell	American composer and pianist
Manitoba	*Canadian province; named by Herman Mann family

Maple Tree	source unknown
Maryland Avenue	*Maryland State
William McKinley	*U.S. president
Meinecke Avenue	*Adolph Meinecke, local businessman and manufacturer
Alexander Mitchell	Local banker and philanthropist
Morgandale	neighborhood/subdivision name
Mound Street	*named for nearby Indian mound
Neeskara	Neeskara Spring, once located on school grounds
Neeskara-Binner Div.	Neeskara Spring; Paul Binner, early Milwaukee educator of deaf
New Road	Source unknown
Ninety-fifth Street	*
Ninth Street	*

Oklahoma Avenue	*
Oklahoma-Binner Div.	*Paul Binner, early Milwaukee educator of deaf
Henry L. Palmer	*local businessman, politician and legislator
Parkview	descriptive name
Emanuel L. Philipp	Local businessman and Wisconsin governor
Franklin Pierce	*U.S. president
Pleasant View	descriptive name
James Whitcomb Riley	Hoosier poet
Seventy-eighth Street	*
William T. Sherman	U.S. general
Siefert	Henry O.R. Siefert, superintendent, MPS
Silver Spring	descriptive name

Sixty-fifth Street   *

Sixty-seventh Street   *

Sixty-sixth Street   *

Story   Alfred Story, Milwaukee pioneer
                                       and philanthropist

Gilbert Stuart   American painter

Thirty-eighth Street   *

Thirty-fifth Street   *

Thirty-first Street   *

Thirty-seventh Street   *

Thirty-sixth Street   *

Tippecanoe   Tippecanoe subdivision and
                                       village

Townsend Street   *Edwin Townsend, early settler
                                       and Milwaukee real estate
                                       pioneer

Trowbridge Street	*William S. Trowbridge, early settler and county surveyor
Twelfth Street	*
Twentieth Street	*
Twenty-first Street	*
Twenty-fourth Street	*
Twenty-seventh Street	*
Victory	source unknown
Vieau	Jacques Vieau, first fur trader on the site of Milwaukee
Walnut Street	*
Warnimont Avenue	*Eugene Warnimont, Milwaukee County Board president
Walt Whitman	American poet
John Greenleaf Whittier	American poet and abolitionist

| Wilson Park | Wilson Park; Woodrow Wilson, U.S. president |
| Wisconsin Avenue | * |

Closed Schools

James Douglas	local architect
James A. Garfield	U.S. president (not to be confused with Garfield Avenue School)
William H. Harrison	U.S. president
Joshua Hathaway	civil engineer, pioneer and public administrator
Mary Hill	elementary principal, MPS
Jones Island	island south of Milwaukee Harbor entrance
John Plankinton	local industrialist
Charles Quentin	board member, state senator and philanthropist
Daniel Webster	statesman

School named after street on which it was located; street named after individual indicated.

CHANGES IN SCHOOL NAMES

Many Milwaukee Public Schools have operated under two or more names. To clarify an otherwise confused record, and thus to facilitate research, the following name changes are listed.

Name of School	Adopted	Former Names
Allen, Walter	1929	Hanover Street to '29; Twelfth District No. 1 to '12
Auer Avenue	1912	Twentieth District No. 4 to '12
Bartlett Avenue	1912	Eighteenth District No 2 to '12
Berger, Victor L.	1931	Third Street to '31; Twenty-first District No. 1 to '12
Boys' Trade and Technical High	1907	Milwaukee School of Trades to '07
*Boys' Trade Annex	1928	Park Street to '28; Fifth District No. 1 to '12
Brown Street	1912	Ninth District No. 2 to '12; Ninth District Primary to '05
Burbank, Luther	1931	Johnson's Woods annexed '26

Cass Street	1912	First District to '12
Clarke Street	1912	Twenty-second District No. 1 to '12
Doerfler, Anna F.	1931	Scott Street to '31; Twenty-third District No. 2 to '12
Dover Street	1912	Seventeenth District No. 1 to '12
Elm	1927	Elm Street to '27; Twenty-second District No. 2 to '12
Field, Eugene	1930	Second Avenue to '30; Eight District No. 3 to '12
Fifth Street	1912	Thirteenth District No. 3 to '12
Forest Home Avenue	1912	Eleventh District No. 1 to '12
Fourth Street	1912	Sixth District No. 1 to '12
Franklin, Benjamin	1923	Franklin Street to '23
Fratney Street	1912	Twenty-first District No. 3 to '12

Gaenslen, Frederick J.	1937	Lapham Park to '37; Lapham School (open air) to '24
Garfield Avenue	1953	North Girls' Junior Trade to '53; Garfield School to '36; Garfield Avenue to '27; Sixth District No. 2 to '12
Grant, U.S.	1929	Grant Street to '29
Green Bay Avenue	1914	Williamsburg to '14
Hayes, R.B.	1930	Fifth Avenue to '30; Fourteenth District No. 2 to '12
Hopkins Street	1912	Twentieth District No. 3 to '12; Twentieth District Primary No. 1
Jefferson, Thomas	1926	Jefferson Street to '26; Seventh District to '12
Juneau, Solomon, Jr./Sr. High	1931	Juneau, Solomon, Junior High to '31; Bluemound Junior High to '30
Kagel, Albert E.	1926	Mineral Street to '26; Eighth District No. 1 to '12

Keefe Avenue	1927	Davis Street to '27
*Kilbourn Junior Trade	1935	Kilbourn Junior Technical High to '35; Byron Kilbourn Pre-Vocational to '31; Pre-Vocational to '23
Kosciuszko Junior High	1957	Kosciuszko Junior Trade to '57; Kosciuszko Junior Technical High to '35; Kosciuszko Pre-Vocational to '23
LaFollette, Robert M.	1931	Ring Street to '31; Twenty-first District No. 2 to '12
Lee	1927	Lee Street to '27; Tenth District NO. 4 to '12
Lincoln Avenue	1949	South Girls' Junior Trade to '49; Lincoln Avenue to '33; Thirteenth Avenue to '17
Lloyd Street	1912	Tenth District No. 1 to '12
Longfellow, H.W.	1930	Sixteenth Avenue to '30; Twenty-third District No. 1 to '12

Maryland Avenue	1912	Eighteenth District No. 1 to '12
McKinley, William B.	1927	Cold Spring Avenue to '27; Fifteenth District No. 1 to '12
Mitchell, Alexander	1930	Eighteenth Avenue to '30; Eleventh District No. 2 to '12
Mound Street	1912	Twelfth District No. 2 to '12
Ninth Street	1912	Tenth District No. 2 to '12
*North Girls' Junior Trade	1935	North Girls' Junior Technical to '35; School for Women's Work to '31; School for Girls to '27
Palmer, Henry L.	1930	Island Avenue to '30; Sixth District No. 3 to '12
Philipp, Emanuel L.	1931	Fifteenth Street to '31
Pierce, Franklin	1956	Pierce Street to '56; Thirteenth District No. 4 to '12; Thirteenth District No. 2 to '12 (annexed to No. 4)

Pulaski, Casimir, High	1933	Southwest High to '33
Riley, James Whitcomb	1930	Greenbush Street to '30
Riverside High	1911	East Division High to '11; East Side High to 1899; High School to 1894
Sherman, William T.	1924	Locust Street to '24
Siefert, H.O.R.	1928	Fourteenth Street to '28; Ninth District No. 1 to '12
*South Girls' Junior Trade	1935	South Girls' Junior Technical High to '35; Pre-Vocational to '31 (transferred to Lincoln Avenue building, '33)
South Division High	1899	South Side High to '99
Story	1927	Thirty-sixth Street to '27
Thirty-eighth Street	1912	Twenty-second District No. 4 to '12
Thirty-first Street	1912	Nineteenth District No. 1 to '12

Thirty-seventh Street	1912	Nineteenth District No. 2 to '12
Trowbridge Street	1912	Seventeenth District No. 2 to '12
Twelfth Street	1912	Twentieth District No. 1 to '12
Twentieth Street	1912	Tenth District No. 3 to '12
Twenty-first Street	1912	Twentieth District No. 2 to '12
Twenty-seventh Street	1912	Fifteenth District No. 2 to '12
Vieau	1927	Walker Street to '27; Fifth District No. 2 to '12
Walker Junior High	1927	Twenty-seventh Avenue to '27
Walnut Street	1912	Nineteenth District No. 3 to '12
West Division High	1899	West Side High to '99
Wisconsin Avenue	1927	Grand Avenue to '27; Sixteenth District No. 2 to '12

CLOSED SCHOOLS/SCHOOLS CONVERTED TO OTHER USES

Former Administration Building (closed 1961)	1914	Prairie Street to '14; Second District No. 1 to '12
Center Street (closed 1966)	1912	Thirteenth District No. 1 to '12
Eighth Street (closed 1967)	1912	Fourth District to '12
Eighteenth Street (closed 1967)	1912	Sixteenth District No. 1 to '12
Harrison, William H. (closed 1931)	1930	Twenty-fifth Avenue to '30 (annexed 1916 as Layton Park)
Highland Avenue (closed 1964)	1927	Prairie Street to '27; Seventh Street to '12; Second District No. 2 to '12
Hill, Mary (closed 1939)	1931	Clybourn Street to '31; Grand Avenue Annex to '14; Sixteenth District Annex No. 2 to '12
Jackson, Andrew (closed 1957)	1927	Detroit Street to '27; Third District to '12
Jones Island (closed 1919)	1914	Park Street Annex to '14; Fifth District No. 3 to '12

Knapp Street (closed 1915)	——	
Lisbon Avenue (closed 1932)	1912	Twenty-second District No. 3 to '12
Madison Street (closed 1940)	1912	Eight District No. 2 to '12
Park Street (closed 1928)	1912	Boys' Trade Annex to '28; Fifth District No. 1 to '12
State Street (closed 1942; reopened 1955–59)	1925	
Twenty-ninth Street (closed 1932)	1928	Garden Acres to '28
Weil Street (closed 1942)	1914	North Pierce Street Annex to '14
Windlake Avenue (closed 1942)	1912	Fourteenth District No. 1 to '12
Wright Street (closed 1942)	1925	Abraham Lincoln (annexed) to '25

*Discontinued

FORMER NAMES WITH LAST KNOWN REFERENCES

Former Name		*Last Known Reference*
District 1	see	Cass Street
District 2-1	see	Former Administration Building
District 2-2	see	Highland Avenue
District 3	see	Andrew Jackson
District 4	see	Eighth Street
District 5-1	see	Boys' Trade Annex
District 5-2	see	Vieau
District 5-3	see	Jones Island
District 6-1	see	Fourth Street
District 6-2	see	Garfield
District 6-3	see	Henry L. Palmer
District 7	see	Thomas Jefferson
District 8-1	see	Albert E. Kagel
District 8-2	see	Madison Street
District 8-3	see	Eugene Field
District 9-1	see	H.O.R. Siefert
District 9-2	see	Brown Street
District 10-1	see	Lloyd Street
District 10-2	see	Ninth Street
District 10-3	see	Twentieth Street

District 10-4	see	Lee
District 11-1	see	Forest Home Avenue
District 11-2	see	Alexander Mitchell
District 12-1	see	Walter Allen
District 12-2	see	Mound Street
District 13-1	see	Center Street
District 13-2	see	Franklin Pierce
District 13-3	see	Fifth Street
District 13-4	see	Franklin Pierce
District 14-1	see	Windlake Avenue
District 14-2	see	Rutherford B. Hayes
District 15-1	see	William McKinley
District 15-2	see	Twenty-seventh Street
District 16-1	see	Eighteenth Street
District 16-2	see	Wisconsin Avenue
District 16-2 Annex	see	Mary Hill
District 17-1	see	Dover Street
District 17-2	see	Trowbridge Street
District 18-1	see	Maryland Avenue
District 18-2	see	Bartlett Avenue
District 19-1	see	Thirty-first Street
District 19-2	see	Thirty-seventh Street
District 19-3	see	Walnut Street

District 20-1	see	Twelfth Street
District 20-2	see	Twenty-first Street
District 20-3	see	Hopkins Street
District 20-4	see	Auer Avenue
District 21-1	see	Victor L. Berger
District 21-2	see	Robert M. LaFollette
District 21-3	see	Fratney Street
District 22-1	see	Clarke Street
District 22-2	see	Elm
District 22-3	see	Lisbon Avenue
District 22-4	see	Thirty-eighth Street
District 23-1	see	Henry W. Longfellow
District 23-2	see	Anna F. Doerfler

Former Name		*Last Known Reference*
Bluemound Junior High	see	Solomon Juneau High
Clybourn Street	see	Mary Hill
Cold Spring Avenue	see	William McKinley
Davis Street	see	Keefe Avenue
Detroit Street	see	Andrew Jackson
East Division High	see	Riverside High
East Side High	see	Riverside High

Eighteenth Avenue	see	Alexander Mitchell
Elm Street	see	Elm
Fifteenth Street	see	Emanuel L. Philipp
Fifth Avenue	see	Rutherford B. Hayes
Fourteenth Street	see	H.O.R. Siefert
Franklin Street	see	Benjamin Franklin
Garden Acres	see	Twenty-ninth Street
Grand Avenue	see	Wisconsin Avenue
Grand Avenue Annex	see	Mary Hill
Grant Street	see	U.S. Grant
Greenbush Street	see	James Whitcomb Riley
Hanover Street	see	Walter Allen
High School	see	Riverside High
Island Avenue	see	Henry L. Palmer
Jefferson Street	see	Thomas Jefferson
Johnson's Woods	see	Luther Burbank
Juneau, Solomon, Junior High	see	Solomon Juneau High
Kilbourn Junior Technical High	see	Kilbourn Junior Trade
Kilbourn, Byron, Pre-Vocational	see	Kilbourn Junior Trade
Kosciuszko Junior Trade	see	Kosciuszko Junior High
Lapham School	see	Frederick J. Gaenslen
Layton Park	see	William H. Harrison
Lee Street	see	Lee

Lincoln, Abraham	see	Wright Street
Locust Street	see	William T. Sherman
Mineral Street	see	Albert E. Kagel
North Girls' Junior Technical High	see	North Girls' Junior Trade
Park Street Annex	see	Jones Island
Pierce Street Annex	see	Weil Street
Prairie Street	see	Administration Building
Ring Street	see	Robert M. LaFollette
School for Girls	see	North Girls' Junior Trade
Scott Street	see	Anna F. Doerfler
Second Avenue	see	Eugene Field
Seventh Street	see	Highland Avenue
Sixteenth Avenue	see	Henry W. Longfellow
South Girls' Pre-Vocational	see	South Girls' Junior Trade
South Girls' Junior Technical High	see	South Girls' Junior Trade
South Side High	see	South Division High
Southwest High	see	Pulaski High
Tenth Street	see	Administration Building
Third Street	see	Victor L. Berger
Thirteenth Avenue	see	Lincoln Avenue
Twenty-fifth Avenue	see	William H. Harrison
Twenty-seventh Avenue	see	George Walker Junior High
Twenty-sixth Street	see	Elm

APPENDIX

Walker Street	see	Vieau
West Side High	see	West Division High
Williamsburg	see	Green Bay Avenue
Women's Work, School for	see	North Girls' Junior Trade

ABOUT THE AUTHOR

Photo by Andy Tarnoff.

Robert Tanzilo is managing editor at OnMilwaukee.com, a daily online city magazine, and created the site SchoolMattersMKE.com. Born and raised in Brooklyn, he attended PS 199, Cunningham JHS 234 and Edward R. Murrow High School. He earned a BA in mass communication at UW-Milwaukee. He lives in Milwaukee with his family and serves on the school governance council at his children's Milwaukee Public School, housed in a vintage building.

Visit us at
www.historypress.net